Feel
AND
Deal
IN ORDER TO
Heal

The Answers Lie Within

MARCELLA ROGERS, LCPC

To contact the author about bulk orders, speaking events, workshops, etc., visit www.answersliewithininc.com.

Paperback ISBN: 979-8-9910697-0-0

Hardback ISBN: 979-8-9910697-1-7

Library of Congress Control Number: 2024925259

Dedication

I dedicate this book to my dear mother, who passed away in June 2015. Though I wish she could be here to witness and celebrate this accomplishment, I know she is always with me in spirit and in my heart. Mama, I miss you deeply. I am grateful for the way you raised and shaped me, molding me into the woman I am today and will continue to become. Thank you for your sacrifices and unwavering belief in me. Through your life, you taught me the importance of feeling, dealing, and healing. I know it wasn't easy for you to express your emotions or confront your own wounds. Mama, I love you.

This book is also dedicated to not only my mother but also to my family, friends, and clients. To my family and my dearest friends, thank you for your unwavering support, help, care, and belief in me, particularly throughout this process. You have been there for me throughout my life, and I am grateful for how you motivated me and how excited you are about my future endeavors.

Finally, I owe an immeasurable debt of gratitude to my **DADDY** – my closest confidant, greatest supporter, and the driving force behind everything I do. Without his unwavering love and encouragement, I wouldn't have the ability to write this book or provide therapy to my clients. I dedicate both my life and this book to **GOD**. Thank you, Daddy, my forever best friend.

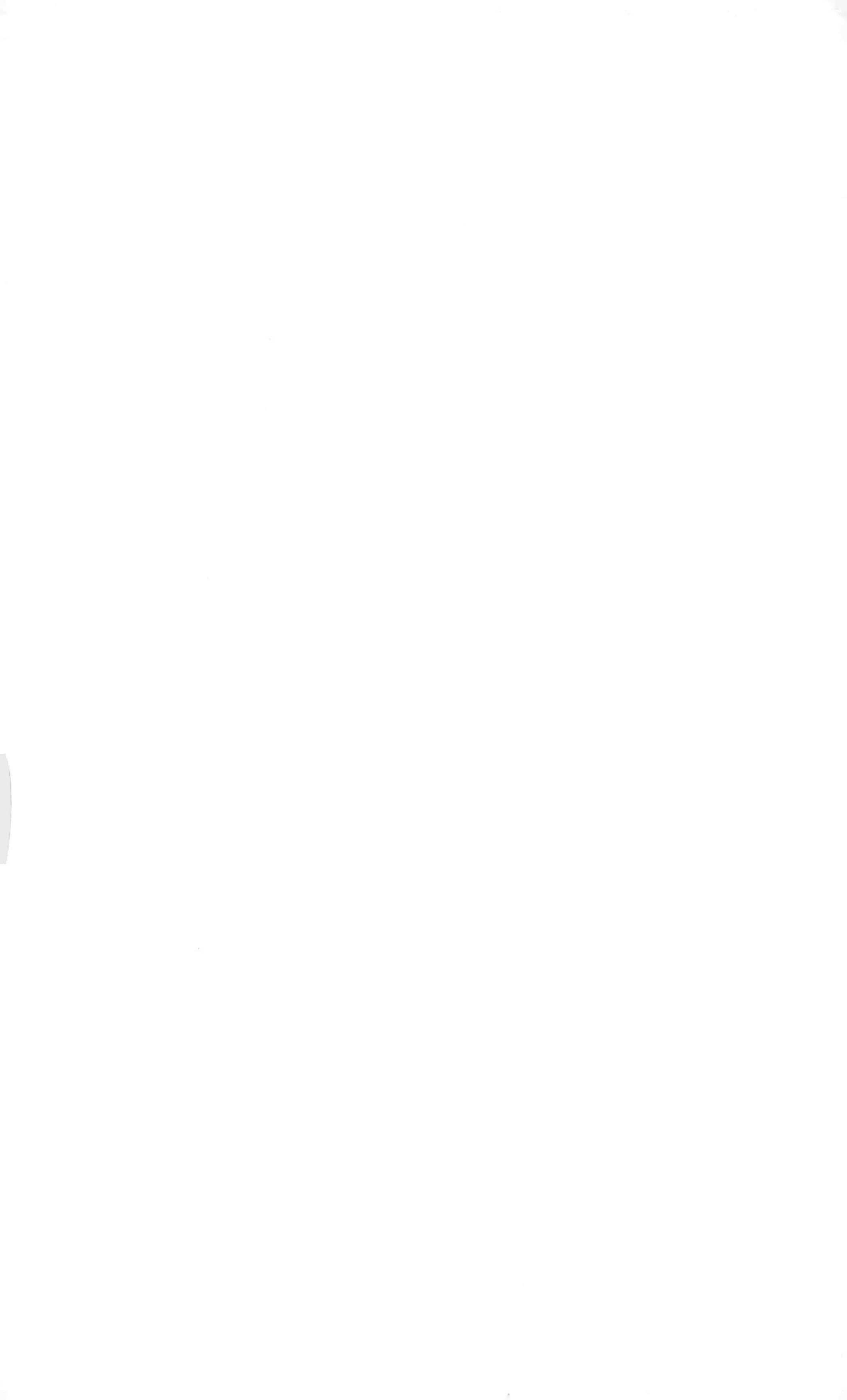

Table of Contents

Introduction

I will admit, there are times when I wish healing was as easy as saying, "1, 2, 3 – BAM – you are healed." I wish it were just that simple. However, I realize that such a belief is rooted in magical thinking. Magical thinking is the notion that our thoughts, actions, and the use of symbols have the power to influence the course of events in our physical world. In essence, it assumes a causal relationship between our inner and personal experiences and the external world.[1]

Dr. Jean Piaget's developmental stages demonstrate that children typically engage in magical thinking due to their limited ability to think logically. This means that we all experience moments where we become captivated by the wonder and possibilities of an event, person, or situation that either hasn't happened yet or may not even come to pass. In such instances, our imaginations can take us on a magical thinking journey. It's worth noting that some of us may rely on magical thinking more than we realize, particularly when dealing with painful experiences or trauma.

While writing this book, I've encountered numerous studies, articles, approaches, and paths toward healing. There was one article in particular that caught my attention: Gavin and Dersch's Five Stages of Healing.[2] These stages include grief and denial, anger, bargaining, depression, and acceptance. Dr. Elisabeth Kübler-Ross initially created and formulated these stages of grief experienced by the dying and their family, but Gavin and Dersch applied them to healing in relationships. I will expound on each of these healing stages.

[1] Neil J. Salkind, ed., *Encyclopedia of Human Development*, 3 vols. (Los Angeles: Sage Publications, 2005).

[2] "Five Stages of Healing," Dersch Family Law, accessed January 2020, https://www. derschfamilylaw.com/family-law/.

1. **Grief And Denial:** This is the first stage of healing from a relationship. It is normal to feel a sense of disbelief or shock after a relationship ends, and it may take some time to come to terms with the reality of the situation, which is called denial. You may feel overwhelmed with emotions such as sadness, fear, and anxiety and may experience physical symptoms such as fatigue, loss of appetite, or trouble sleeping. It can be the result of desertion and rejection. No matter how bad the relationship might have been, a sense of loss exists. Before learning to accept your grief, you will probably deny your loss.

2. **Anger:** This is the second stage of healing from a relationship. During this stage, you may feel angry about the way the relationship ended or about the circumstances that led to the break-up. You may also feel angry at yourself, your ex-partner, or others involved in the situation, asking, "Why me?" It is important to remember that anger is a normal part of the healing process and recognizing anger helps you move on to the next stage. It is vital to find healthy ways to express and cope with your anger.

3. **Bargaining:** This is the third stage of healing from a relationship. During this stage, you may find yourself trying to negotiate or make deals with your ex-partner in an attempt to salvage the relationship. For example, you may say, "I promise I won't hurt you again if you give me another chance," or "I won't go through the divorce if you will just try counseling." You may also try to bargain with yourself, making promises or setting unrealistic expectations for how you will feel in the future. It's important to recognize that bargaining is a normal part of the process, but ultimately, it is vital to focus on what's best for your own well-being.

4. **Depression:** This is the fourth stage of healing from a relationship, which is unexpressed anger turned inward. During this stage, you may feel a sense of sadness or

hopelessness about the situation. You may experience exhaustion, suffer from low self-esteem, and feel emptiness, loneliness, isolation, or loss of interest in things you used to enjoy. It is important to take care of yourself by expressing your emotions and seeking professional help if necessary.

5. **Acceptance:** This is the fifth and final stage of healing from a relationship. During this stage, you may begin to feel a sense of peace and closure about the relationship. You recognize the relationship is over and it's time to move on. It's important to remember that acceptance is not the same as forgetting or ignoring what happened in the relationship; rather, it's about acknowledging the reality of the situation and finding a way to move forward. It is when your faith develops and your growth follows.

According to this approach, a crisis can serve as a catalyst to break old patterns and initiate transformative changes. However, it is crucial to allow sufficient time for healing and be willing to become a healed individual. Gavin and Dersch emphasized the importance of identifying one's emotional needs and setting realistic goals to achieve progress. It is essential to ask oneself where one wants to be in a month or a year from now.

Why This Book?

You may be wondering why I am writing this book if there are already established stages of healing. Through my clinical practice and working with countless individuals, I have discovered certain steps that have proven effective in facilitating healing. Drawing on my personal experiences, I have created a **guide** to healing that I have used in my work with my clients. This guide builds on the established stages of healing and offers practical, actionable steps that individuals can take to progress toward emotional recovery.

I believe that sharing our personal experiences and the knowledge we have gained can be a powerful tool for helping others. In this book, I am sharing what I have learned and what has been helpful and rewarding for myself and the many people who trusted me on their healing journey. With my clients' permission, I will also share some of their stories and experiences. To protect their privacy and confidentiality, I have changed their names and identifying details and modified some details of their stories. I have not disclosed any client's story in its entirety. It is my hope that these stories will inspire and encourage others who may be going through similar struggles.

The world would be a better place with less pain, anger, and shame and more happiness and peace if there was a clear step-by-step process for healing. Despite the myriad of articles, books, modules, and treatments claiming to offer the ultimate guide to healing, many people still struggle with emotional wounds and brokenness.

The aim of this book is to provide hands-on material for individuals seeking to **start** and embark on the journey of healing. I am not claiming that this book is the cure or the best treatment for every type of emotional pain, loss, or self-hatred. Rather, my intention is to help readers **begin** the venture toward healing, which is something that we all need in our lives. WE ALL NEED HEALING.

My observations during my clinical work with clients served as the motivation for the development of this book. Many of them were avoiding their emotions and not dealing with the root cause of their pain. I realized the importance of helping them identify and acknowledge their feelings and give themselves permission to feel the pain. I believe that learning how to feel and validate our emotions is an essential step toward healing, and I hope that this book will help readers do just that and know that our feelings are real.

Why Focus on Emotions

You might be curious about the reason why I emphasize the importance of our emotions. I cannot stress enough how vital it is to acknowledge and validate our feelings. As someone who is passionate about healing, I need you to understand just how indispensable you are to me, especially your feelings: **"YOU ARE VALUABLE TO ME."**

I encourage my clients to be present with their emotions by staying in the moment, sitting with them, and processing them. When I ask my clients how they are feeling, I also encourage them to explain the emotion and not avoid or ignore it. I understand that some of you may feel uncomfortable or uneasy with this process, but I assure you that as we continue, it will become more natural and less foreign. Although this may be challenging, it is crucial to ask ourselves whether ignoring or avoiding our emotions is truly working for us. The fact that you are here reading this book suggests you already know the answer.

I believe people seek counseling because what worked for them in the past is no longer effective. In other words, what was working for them previously isn't working for them anymore. Some people come to therapy to find and explore other effective ways that will work. Therefore, I ask my clients for permission to take them out of their comfort zone and help them process their emotions. This involves being present, focusing on the "here and now," and not self-medicating or running away from their feelings.

What does this look like? Many years ago, I was in a session with a client named Rosie. She was visibly upset and crying. I asked her, "How are you feeling? And please identify your feelings." As tears streamed down her face, leaving a rosy tint on her cheeks, I validated her struggle and how difficult it was for her to verbalize her feelings. I encouraged her to allow herself to feel the pain, sadness, disappointment, and sorrow. She said, "I don't know how I feel. I don't know how to feel. I don't want to feel those things. I just can't. Heck, I'm not weak." Despite expressing that she was struggling with identifying and acknowledging how she actually felt, I reassured her that it was okay to have a hard time and that she was safe to sit with those emotions and release them. I empathized with her agony and acknowledged the hurt she was experiencing by telling her, "I see your hurt and pain."

As she opened up and became vulnerable, I inquired about how she had coped with pain, hurt, and disappointment in the past. After calming down, she revealed, "I just move on. That's how I deal." It struck me that this was a pervasive societal problem – we've all been taught to "JUST MOVE ON' (how familiar is that?). I elaborated on the importance of being able to distinguish between moving on and dealing.

Moving on is similar to the "microwave mentality" that is all too common these days. We want a quick fix for our food, so we throw it into the microwave and move on. The prepared food is quickly consumed. Unfortunately, we tend to treat our lives the same way. We seek instant gratification and fast results, and we want to be rewarded immediately. We often overlook our problems and those of others, wanting to move on to the next thing without addressing the underlying issues.

It's like walking into your house and coming across a puddle of water. You have two options: you can simply step over it and keep walking, or you can take the time to find a mop and clean it up. In our lives, we often have problems that we tend to step over instead of taking the time to deal with them by addressing them. It's important that we learn to deal with our wounds by stopping and taking a moment to talk about the problem, process our issues and emotions, acknowledge the hurt, and make a decision about what to do next.

During the session, I observed Rosie's expression change from astonishment to relief as she allowed herself to feel her emotions. Despite feeling uncomfortable, she also felt "better" after expressing her feelings. She revealed how hurt, sad, and devastated she was and that it was a relief to share these emotions with someone. She reported that it was the first time she had ever shared these feelings with anyone. It was validating for her to know that it was okay to feel and express them.

Rosie's story underlines why it is essential to acknowledge, recognize, and explore why we feel a certain way and what we have felt in situations or experiences that we have faced. These can include being abandoned, going through a break-up, experiencing heartache, confusion, the death of a loved one, trauma, hurt by a religious institution, being a victim of a crime or infidelity, disappointment, abandonment, a layoff or getting fired, divorce, health issues, eviction, financial changes, betrayal, loneliness, self-doubt, neglected, and abused physically, sexually, mentally, emotionally, psychologically, and verbally. The list of potential harms and wounds that inflict emotional injuries is endless, and healing is crucial.

Just like many of you, I have been hurt personally in various ways due to my multiple roles and responsibilities. As a mother, daughter, girlfriend, lover, ex-wife, sister, entrepreneur, employee, employer, aunt, counselor, and an involved church member, I have faced different challenges that have led me to seek healing. I too have experienced heartaches, the deaths of loved ones, various types of losses, disappointments, betrayals, and other adversities that have contributed to my own journey of healing. I am proud to say that my personal and professional experiences have equipped me to create this book and share my knowledge with you.

My Hopes for My Readers

I hope my book provides a useful and applicable formula for healing that empowers individuals to become more authentic and transparent with themselves and others. By identifying and embracing our truth, we can walk confidently on a path toward a healthier and more genuine sense of self. Through the power of walking, talking, and living in our **TRUTH**, we can achieve a sense of freedom and self-awareness, leading us to a more fulfilling life.

My intention and desire are to convey to you the significance of healing, particularly when it comes to our emotions. My earnest wish is that you find the courage to confront your feelings, even if it makes you uncomfortable, and initiate the healing process. I strongly encourage you to be able to be still, sit with your feelings, and allow yourself to feel discomfort. By gaining a deeper understanding of how essential it is to acknowledge and address our emotions, I hope we can move away from the tendency to avoid, ignore, or bypass them. It is my goal to give ourselves the chance to confront our emotions and ultimately **FEEL, DEAL, and HEAL**.

By the time you finish reading this book, you will have a deeper understanding of three crucial principles of healing. This knowledge will provide you with a sense of release, freedom, and liberation, followed by self-consciousness and ultimately comfort. You will learn how to live fully, stay in the present, and love deeply by embracing the process of feeling and dealing with your emotions. Through this journey, you will realize the transformative power of healing.

Chapter 1
The Importance of Healing

Who Needs to Heal?

EVERYBODY needs to heal. It's important to recognize that healing is a universal need. No one is exempt from the need to heal, regardless of their background, status, or experiences. Whether you've been through trauma, made mistakes, or simply have dealt with challenges in your life, *YOU NEED HEALING*. Healing is not just for those who have experienced extreme trauma; it's for anyone who wants to live a more fulfilled, authentic, and joyful life. The process of healing requires vulnerability, honesty, and courage, but it's worth it in the end. By taking the time to heal, you can release the pain of the past and embrace a brighter future.

Every individual, regardless of their position or role in society, has experienced pain and hurt at some point in their lives. None of us are excused from the need for healing. Whether it is the leaders of nations, governors, or our closest friends and family members, we have all encountered moments of hurt.

Let's consider a range of individuals who are in need of healing. For instance, some believe in the societal norm of "just moving on" and "getting over it." They require healing. Women who have had their rights infringed upon by the government need healing. A young boy who was given up for adoption and a little girl who lost her mother at the age of six months both require healing.

The need for healing extends to an elderly man who lost his wife to COVID-19 and an elderly woman who has been coping with the death of her husband for the past ten years. A mother whose son was tragically murdered while walking home from school and a father who passed away before having the chance to meet his newborn baby due to a miscarriage at 26 weeks both need healing.

A teenage boy who discovered that his first love, high school sweetheart, cheated on him requires healing. A teenage girl who put in intense effort and attended various tryouts, but didn't make it onto the basketball team and an employee who was laid off right before the holidays need healing. The grandparent who is unable to see their grandchildren due to issues with the parents requires healing.

Staff members facing discrimination due to their sexual preference and orientation need to embark on a healing journey. The state trooper who attempted suicide requires healing, as does his family. The parents who experienced the devastating loss of their daughter due to medical complications at the hospital need healing. The doctor who has witnessed several patients pass away needs healing, given the emotional toll such experiences can take. A social worker who was betrayed by a coworker requires healing to address the resulting emotional wounds.

Individuals who have experienced various forms of abuse within their family dynamics need healing. This includes a sister who was touched inappropriately by her brother during childhood and a brother who was forced to engage in unwanted sexual acts with his sister. The husband who received the sudden news of his wife's desire for divorce without any prior indication or warning also needs healing.

A client who was hurt by their therapist and a manager facing retaliation and disrespect from subordinates require healing. The spouse or partner who discovers that their significant other is expecting a baby or has already had a child with someone else needs healing. The person whose parents constantly belittle them and undermine their self-worth needs healing, as does the student who has been subjected to disrespectful behavior, name-calling, and public humiliation by their teacher.

These examples illustrate the diverse range of individuals who can benefit from healing, encompassing different experiences and emotions. In each of these cases, healing is crucial for individuals to address their emotional wounds, find inner strength, and move forward toward a healthier state of being.

Imagine someone you know personally who needs healing due to pain, hurt, and disappointment they have experienced. Consider their conversations and how they express their emotions or potentially act out their agony, hurt, and dissatisfaction toward you.

Reflect on the state of the world we currently live in. Take notice of senseless crime, loss of life, acts of violence, natural disasters like wildfires, earthquakes, hurricanes, and tornadoes, as well as the challenges posed by pandemics, wars, pollution, and climate change, among others. All of these factors contribute to a world in dire need of healing. It extends beyond individual experiences to encompass the collective healing of our planet and society as a whole. We all yearn for healing to address the pain, wounds, and challenges surrounding us.

Healing is an overall need that affects everyone. Recognizing the need for healing on personal, societal, and global levels is the first step toward initiating positive change. By fostering empathy, understanding, and compassion, we can actively work toward healing ourselves, supporting others in their healing journeys, and contributing to the healing of our world. It is through collective efforts and a shared commitment to healing that we can create a better future, a world that is more peaceful, harmonious, and sustainable for everyone.

We cannot continue to ignore the fact that everyone is impacted by some form of pain or trauma that requires healing. It is essential that we take healing seriously and work towards creating a culture that values and prioritizes it. By acknowledging and addressing our pain, we can begin to heal and live healthier, happier, and more fulfilling lives.

Why Do We Hesitate to Heal?

If you find yourself hesitant or uncertain about the healing process, have you considered the potential consequences of allowing your wounds to heal? How the world we live in would be impacted if people embraced the healing journey?

Let's ponder a few questions: What transformations would occur if you embarked on your own healing journey? How might things have unfolded if your mother, father, or caretaker had chosen to heal? And what lies ahead if you take the first step in your healing process?

Understanding your fears and concerns is crucial. What is it that you fear about the healing process? What fears drive others to avoid healing? What exactly are people trying to evade? What aspects of life do you hesitate to confront or face head-on? By delving into these questions, we can gain a deeper understanding of your hesitations and fears surrounding healing, allowing for a more meaningful exploration of the healing process and its potential to impact your personal growth and the world around us.

Society has affected certain beliefs and teachings about healing, shaping our understanding of this process. We have been taught the "rights and wrongs" of how to heal through education, books, articles, podcasts, social media, the news, commercials, and the "norms" of the world. People have been criticized or ridiculed about how "vulnerable" they appear.

Think about what society has taught us. Explore how extensive our knowledge is regarding healing based on societal norms. Reflect on your understanding of how to heal and how you personally experienced healing in the past. Compare your belief about your capacity to heal to what people around you say and do. Look at the impact of how judging each other influences our views about who deserves to heal or not. Doing so will help you be open to what wounds you actually carry versus what you believe society tells you or says about it.

Society has provided various perspectives on healing, ranging from physical recovery to the passage of time. Societal healing involves addressing systemic issues, fostering understanding and empathy, promoting inclusivity, and working toward creating a more harmonious and equitable society.

However, true healing often involves delving into the underlying causes of pain, acknowledging and processing emotions, and cultivating self-awareness. It is an individual and unique journey for each person. It's important to process and evaluate what society says about healing and how it has changed how you heal.

Over the past two decades, I have delved into the depths of this topic, both personally and professionally, working closely with individuals to identify, encourage, and support them throughout their healing journeys. I have witnessed the power of healing and its transformative effects on individuals' lives. It is a deeply personal journey for each person, and my role has been to offer guidance, empathy, and assistance along the way.

I recognize that healing encompasses diverse aspects, including physical, emotional, and spiritual dimensions. It involves understanding the roots of pain, embracing vulnerability, and finding inner strength. It requires acknowledging past traumas, processing difficult emotions, and fostering self-compassion.

As we explore the realm of healing, there will always be new insights to uncover, additional questions to ponder, and different paths to follow. Healing is a multifaceted, ongoing, and ever-expanding process in which we gain insights and share experiences. It is through this ongoing exploration that we can deepen our understanding and enhance our ability to support others in their healing endeavors.

Healing can have a profound impact on individual well-being, especially when someone allows themselves to heal. Whether it is physical, emotional, or psychological, healing allows individuals to address and resolve past traumas, pain, and negative experiences. It enables personal growth, self-discovery, and the development of healthier coping mechanisms. Individuals often experience a sense of liberation, inner peace, and increased self-awareness. This can lead to positive changes in their relationships as they are better able to connect with others on a deeper level. Healing also empowers individuals to break free from patterns of self-destructive behavior, allowing them to make healthier choices and live more fulfilling lives.

If someone were to undergo the healing process, they might experience a release of emotional baggage, a greater capacity for joy and love, and an enhanced ability to navigate life's challenges with resilience. This in turn would positively influence their relationships, enabling deeper connections and healthier interactions. Healing empowers individuals to get away from self-defeating patterns and make choices that enhance their well-being and fulfillment. It can contribute to personal transformation and a more positive outlook on life. People who allow themselves to address and resolve their past traumas, tragedies, and negative experiences find themselves on a path to personal growth and self-discovery.

While the healing process can be challenging, frightening, and daunting, it offers immense rewards. It requires individuals to confront their pain, and vulnerability, and face difficult emotions or memories. Fear of the unknown, fear of reliving past traumas, and resistance to change often deter people from embarking on their healing journey. People may also avoid healing because they are comfortable with their current state, even if it is painful or dysfunctional. After all, it is familiar and offers a sense of security. Change can be intimidating, and the process of healing often involves stepping out of one's comfort zone and embracing vulnerability.

Ultimately, embracing healing is a courageous and transformative choice. The decision to heal is a personal one. It demands and requires courage, self-reflection, and a willingness to confront the past and embrace change. The healing process can lead to profound growth, improved well-being, and more positive interactions with others. It opens doors to a life of greater authenticity, fulfillment, and the opportunity to create a positive impact.

What Science Says About Healing

According to the World Health Organization, in 2002, it was estimated that more than 80% of the world's population could benefit from traditional healing modalities, highlighting the widespread need for healing across various communities and cultures.[3] A study conducted by Crawford, Sparber, and Jonas between 1955 and 2001 examined the quality of research on hands-on versus distance healing.[4] Out of 90 identified studies, 45 were conducted in clinical settings and 45 in laboratory settings. The findings indicated that 71% of the clinical studies and 62% of the laboratory studies reported positive outcomes. Moreover, the overall internal validity for the studies on distance healing was reported to be 75% for clinical investigations and 81% for laboratory investigations. Healing is clearly effective in a variety of contexts.

Individuals who have experienced healing often report improvements in multiple aspects of their lives. Relationships, overall happiness, work, and productivity are among the areas where positive changes have been observed. A study involving 300 clients with diverse ailments provided additional evidence supporting the benefits of healing.[5] This study demonstrated positive impacts on both psychological and physical functioning. The findings of this study revealed that a significant number of individuals with an illness duration of over one year reported substantial improvements after just

[3] *WHO Traditional Medicine Strategy 2002-2005* (Geneva, Switzerland: World Health Organization, 2002), https://www.who.int/publications/i/item/WHO-EDM-TRM-2002.1.

[4] Cindy C. Crawford, Andrew G. Sparber, and Wayne B. Jonas, "A Systematic Review of the Quality of Research on Hands-On and Distance Healing: Clinical and Lab-oratory Studies," *Alternative Therapies In Health And Medicine 9 (2003)*: A96–104, https://pubmed.ncbi.nlm.nih.gov/12776468/.

[5] Chittaranjan Andrade and Rajiv Radhakrishnan, "Prayer and Healing: A Medical and Scientific Perspective on Randomized Controlled Trials," Indian Journal of Psychiatry 51, no. 4 (October–December, 2009): 247–253, doi: 10.4103/0019-5545.58288.

four healing sessions conducted for 4 to 6 weeks. Notably, those with the most severe symptoms at the beginning of the study showed the greatest improvements in their well-being.

These results offer strong circumstantial evidence suggesting the efficacy of healing modalities in promoting positive changes in individuals' overall functioning. It indicates that even a relatively short duration of healing sessions can lead to significant benefits, particularly for those experiencing long-term or severe symptoms. Additional research is necessary to explore the specific mechanisms and long-term effects of healing practices on various ailments. Nonetheless, these findings highlight the potential of healing as a valuable approach to enhancing psychological and physical well-being in individuals.

One of the primary phases of healing, as defined by scientists, is homeostasis. This phase marks the beginning of the response to an injury, aimed at stopping bleeding and initiating the repair process. During homeostasis, the body activates its emergency repair system, primarily the blood clotting system, to form a protective barrier and prevent further loss of blood. In this sense, if we apply the concept of homeostasis to emotional or psychological wounds, we can draw parallels to the need for recognizing and acknowledging the onset of the hurt and trauma.

Just as the body instinctively responds to physical injuries to restore balance and initiate healing, it is important for individuals to identify and acknowledge their emotional wounds. Recognizing and acknowledging these wounds is an essential first step toward initiating the healing process for the heart and mind.

Here are some ways to apply the concept of homeostasis to emotional healing:

1. **Acknowledge the Emotional Wound:** The first step is to acknowledge and recognize the emotional wound. This involves being honest with yourself about the pain, trauma, or hurt you have experienced and accepting its existence.

2. **Create a Safe Environment:** Just as the body creates a protective barrier during homeostasis, it is important to establish a safe and supportive environment for emotional healing. This can involve seeking out trusted friends, family members, or professionals who can provide a nurturing and non-judgmental space for you to express your feelings and experiences.

3. **Stop the "Bleeding":** In the context of emotional healing, "bleeding" refers to any ongoing sources of distress or triggers that exacerbate the emotional wound. Identify and address these factors, whether they are unhealthy relationships, negative thought patterns, or harmful behaviors. Take steps to remove or minimize these influences to create a more stable and healing environment.

4. **Seek Emotional Support:** Just as the body relies on the blood clotting system during homeostasis, seek out emotional support systems. This can include therapy, counseling, support groups, or talking to trusted individuals who can provide guidance, empathy, and validation during the healing process.

5. **Develop Self-Care Practices:** Self-care plays a vital role in restoring emotional balance. Engage in activities that promote your well-being, such as exercise, mindfulness, journaling, creative expression, or engaging in hobbies that bring you happiness. Prioritize self-care as a way to support your emotional healing.

6. **Allow Time for Healing:** Just as physical healing takes time, emotional healing is a process that requires patience and self-compassion. Give yourself permission to grieve, process emotions, and gradually work through the healing journey at your own pace.

By understanding the concept of homeostasis in the context of emotional healing, individuals can begin to address the trauma and wounds they have experienced. This recognition and acknowledgment paves the way for further phases of healing, such as repair, regeneration, and ultimately, restoration of well-being.

It is worth noting that the healing process, whether physical or emotional, is complex and multifaceted. While the concept of homeostasis provides a framework for understanding the initial phase of healing, it is important to seek professional guidance and support to navigate the subsequent stages of healing and develop effective coping strategies. Healing emotional wounds is a deeply personal journey, and each individual's process may differ. With time, support, and self-care, it is possible to restore emotional balance and wellness.

The Principles Guiding Healing

During my healing research, I discovered the work of William Vernes, who delved into the healing process and identified the seven key principles that underpin the healing ethos.[6] Before going deeper into Vernes' principles, it's important to understand the definition of ethos, which refers to the fundamental values and aspirations of culture, era, or community. Vernes' medical model of healing closely aligns with key aliments that I believe are essential in helping individuals on their journey. He looked at each of his patients individually, not just focusing on the medical problem. Many people have expressed how medical staff put a label on them and treat them accordingly. They feel as if they are dehumanized when the provider's bedside manner isn't personal and they aren't connected to the patient.

It is important for me to make sure that every client I see feels seen and heard. I often say, when the doctor says you have diabetes, do you walk around and say, "Hi, my name is Diabetes?" Our identity isn't solely based on our medical conditions. We sometimes need help to understand how we are treated during this time may have a huge effect on our recovery.

---

[6] William B. Ventres, "Healing," *The Annals of Family Medicine* 14, no. 1 (January 2016): 76–78, doi: 10.1370/afm.1889.

Vernes' principles reflect how I approach the healing process with my clients:

1. **Dignity:** Each patient is regarded as a person of inherent worth, deserving respect, time, and attention. Vernes recognizes the unity of body, mind, and soul in individuals and acknowledges their unique histories, aspirations, and experiences with both success and failure. Treating others, including oneself, with dignity is crucial for the healing process.

2. **Authenticity:** Vernes emphasizes the importance of being true to oneself in medical appointments. By embracing his own humanity, he brings qualities such as curiosity, empathy, and passion to his interactions with patients, contributing to the healing process.

3. **Integrity:** This principle involves connecting dignity and authenticity. It entails honestly perceiving reality through a holistic understanding of physical, psychological, social, and existential aspects. Combining scientific advancements with an awareness of suffering leads to effective treatment plans and improved outcomes. What we believe in, our morals, and values are essential in how we approach healing.

4. **Transparency:** Vernes promotes openness in healing encounters. Actively listening, asking questions with a probe-and-pause style, and acknowledging differing opinions fosters collaborative decision-making, helping to clarify concerns, explore options, and reach suitable solutions.

5. **Solidarity:** Vernes works with, rather than just for, his patients, recognizing the interconnectedness of individuals in an interdependent world. By approaching care without judgment and with relaxed confidence and humility, he cultivates healing relationships that benefit both himself and his patients.

6. **Generosity:** This principle entails the willingness to give of one's time, resources, and self. Vernes encourages altruism and highlights the importance of offering competent care. In return, he receives trust and respect, fostering a reciprocal sense of gratitude and creating opportunities for mutual help.

7. **Resiliency:** Vernes emphasizes the capacity to rebound from setbacks and learn from mistakes. Recognizing errors in knowledge or judgment, being honest about limitations, and embracing forgiveness contribute to personal growth, wisdom, and the overall healing process.

These seven ethos principles by William Vernes provide a framework for understanding and approaching healing, guiding individuals in their own journeys, and offering the potential to alleviate suffering.

First Steps Toward Healing

I have a favor to ask each of you right now. Take a moment to close your eyes and reflect on yourself. I want you to think about a particular relationship, friendship, disappointment, heartbreak, fear, or experience of loss that you encountered.

Ask yourself, "Have I recovered from that experience? Have I allowed myself to fully address and navigate through that emotional pain?"

After pausing and taking a breath, with your eyes open describe and articulate your observations and thoughts. Please share what caught your attention or crossed your mind during this experience. List what you saw and thought about.

____

____

____

____

____

____

____

____

____

____

Let us now dig deeper. Take a moment to jot down the wounds you have experienced, whether stemming from trauma, hurt, pain, disappointment, or the loss of loved ones.

____

____

____

____

____

____

____

____

Let us embark on the journey of healing by acknowledging and addressing your wounds. Together, we will identify the ones you are ready to deal with in order to heal from them.

Chapter 2

The Myth of "Get Over It"

Why Do We Need to Heal?

DURING a recent session with a client named Bobby, the topic of his trust issues arose. He shared that he had been betrayed by his high school sweetheart, an experience that still lingered in his heart. Bobby expressed his desire to move on from the pain caused by his ex-partner's affair with his best friend, feeling as though he had wasted precious years of his life. His exact statement was, "I just want to get over her breaking my heart by sleeping with my best friend. I wasted so much of my time and some good years of my life. *I just want to get over it.*"

This scenario resonates with many of us who have experienced heartbreak and adopted the belief that we simply need to just "get over it." How many of us can relate to the statement, "We **wasted** our time." It is common for us to perceive our past hurts, pains, and relationships as time wasted, which can keep us feeling trapped and stagnant. We often find ourselves feeling stuck. This perception of wasted time creates a mental prison, preventing us from viewing our experiences as valuable learning opportunities. I believe we put our lives in a box with many restrictions instead of looking at relationships as learning experiences. I often refer to them as learning curves.

Many people often advise us to simply *"move on"* and *"get over it."* However, years later, we find ourselves feeling miserable, hurt, and experiencing a sense of emptiness. We may struggle with unexplained mood swings, restlessness, uneasiness, and heightened sensitivity, among other emotions. Some people choose to avoid these emotions altogether by suppressing any emotional reactions and solely focusing on behavioral responses. Consequently, they make statements like, "I don't like feeling like this or that. I dislike feeling this way. I don't know how to feel. Feeling, what's that? I don't have those types of feelings. I ignore them. I'm not weak. I don't like being vulnerable. Vulnerability is weak. What's the point, nothing changes. I'm too busy to go there. I don't have time. I'm good. I have to make sure everyone else is okay."

With all of those excuses, people may even claim not to possess certain emotions, intentionally ignoring them, as they associate vulnerability with weakness. They question the purpose of going deeper into their feelings, believing that nothing will change. They may feel too busy to explore their emotions, prioritizing the well-being of others over their own. If this resonates with you, then understanding the importance and necessity of healing becomes crucial.

Or maybe your response was more like what Bobby said. I conveyed to Bobby that "healing from hurt" is more appropriate than simply "getting over it." This notion seemed to surprise him, and he responded by saying, "I don't know how to do that because I wasn't taught *that* or encouraged by society to do that. I really don't know how to heal. I just get over it." This sentiment may resonate with many of you who can relate to saying, "I don't know how to X." If it does, then understanding the importance and necessity of healing is crucial for you too.

Understanding the Importance of Healing

When our bodies are injured, how do we effectively treat physical wounds? Think about your most recent experience with a wound Where is the wound located? How did you go about treating it? What measures did you take to protect it? It's good that you experienced the initial sting, acknowledging the pain and discomfort it brought. Fortunately, over time, the pain subsided, and the wound had successfully healed. You feel better and a sense of improvement.

But consider the consequences of neglecting a wound. It can prolong the true healing process, become infected, or even lead to sepsis. Now, there are those who believe wounds can heal on their own. While that may hold true for certain wounds, there are cases where additional measures such as alcohol, peroxide, ointment, stitches, surgery, or other treatments are necessary. Failing to properly treat a wound can result in the development of an infection. Consequently, the problem becomes more severe, deeper, and potentially life-threatening.

The same principle applies to our emotional, spiritual, mental, and psychological wounds. I understand that many of us may be going through difficult times. None of us are immune to life's struggles. Life can throw unexpected curveballs at us, some fast, some slow, and some hard. If you are like me, you might have encountered numerous losses, hurts, disappointments, betrayals, and tragedies that have left you without proper healing. These experiences and life in general have left deep-rooted wounds within us. Many of us carry these unaddressed wounds, which have inevitably resulted in lasting scars that are visible, while others remain hidden.

Some visible scars manifest in various forms, such as alcoholism and excessive marijuana use, engaging in verbal and physical aggression toward oneself and others, bullet wounds, self-inflicted scratches, and superficial marks from biting nails excessively – just to name a few examples. On the other hand, the hidden invisible scars may manifest as sadness, depression, disappointment, fear, loneliness, discouragement, self-doubt, self-hatred, a sense of emptiness, numbness, bleakness, anger, greed, and a persistent feeling of "not feeling good enough" along with inadequacy, among others.

These internal scars require dedicated attention and time to facilitate their healing. Their existence creates numerous reasons why it is essential to address and heal our internal wounds. And like physical wounds, if we neglect or fail to address our emotional wounds, hurts, and brokenness, we run the risk of becoming stuck and stagnant, and experiencing physical, mental, psychological, and emotional distress.

Unresolved hurts can manifest into deeper internal issues that continue to fester and exacerbate our pain. Unfortunately, this can lead to self-harm, harm to others, dysfunctionality, substance abuse, excessive spending, gambling, unhealthy eating patterns (often referred to as emotional eating), and intense anger, among other manifestations.

The reasons behind our emotional pain may vary widely, such as past relationships, childhood experiences, letdowns, feeling forgotten, invisible, unimportant, not good enough, and abandoned through death, break ups, disappearance or "ghosted," left, neglect, relocation, and avoidance.

In order to initiate the healing process, it is critical to first identify the wounds, hurts, traumas, or pains that exist. Without knowing what needs healing, it becomes difficult to ask for assistance in the healing journey or to understand the significance of the process. It is of utmost importance to take time to acknowledge, observe, and pinpoint the sources and individuals from which we need healing.

Our wounds originate from various sources, such as neglect, tragedy, and trauma. These experiences leave behind visible and internal scars that can manifest in different forms. The sources of the scars we carry may extend beyond the physical realm, encompassing the realms of our mental, emotional, spiritual, and psychological well-being. It is crucial to explore the complex nature of these sources to gain a comprehensive understanding.

For instance, each of us carries within us fragments that are broken, such as our hearts, self-esteem, sense of worth, self-identity, and feelings of security. We bear bruises from life's trials and tribulations, marked by stains, blemishes, and voids stemming from disappointments, betrayals, heartaches, losses, intentional and unintentional inflictions of pain, offenses, and personal battles. Trust issues may arise from various sources, be it family, ourselves, friends, teachers, religious institutions, loved ones, or figures of authority. Many of us have encountered experiences of rejection, neglect, and abandonment.

These experiences can manifest in overt ways, with tangible events unfolding before our eyes. Witnessing traumatic events such as accidents, natural disasters, violent incidents, abuse, grieving the death of a close friend, family member, or pet, and the dissolution of a marriage or a significant romantic relationship can lead to emotional wounds. So can coping with a chronic illness or living with a disability, trying to navigate changes in one's health, lifestyle, and self-perception. Other events might involve interpersonal issues where we may struggle with forming and maintaining healthy relationships. We might exhibit difficulties in trusting others, fear of intimacy, or challenges in expressing emotions. We may experience physical symptoms from emotional distress, which can manifest into headaches, digestive issues, or chronic pain. Some of us may have mental health issues like depression and anxiety, persistent feelings of sadness, hopelessness, or excessive worry.

Conversely, they can be covert, very rooted in internal emotions and experiences where neglect or abandonment may not have actually occurred but felt as if they did. For instance, how we manage and control our emotions and how we cognitively process information and situations is key. Our conflict resolution and problem-solving abilities are another example because they reflect how we strategize and plan solutions mentally. We may engage in self-reflection and internal dialogue, having deep thoughts about ourselves and others and how our values and experiences are affected. We may experience being self-critical, constantly berating ourselves internally as we aim for perfectionism in which we set unrealistic high standards for ourselves can result in emotional and chronic stress and a fear of failure. Another example is daydreaming and visualizing scenarios when we allow our minds to wander into imagination, creating mental images, and situations or fantasizing. Some of us may experience rumination when we repeatedly dwell on negative thoughts or experiences without resolution, which can lead to negative self-talk. We may suppress our emotions rather than express them, which can lead to emotional buildup and eventually outburst. Some people may overthink and catastrophize when they always expect the worst possible outcomes and imagine the worst-case scenarios. Or they may become dependent on external validation, relying solely on approval from others.

It is crucial to have a good understanding of both physical experiences and the emotional, internal ones because both produce emotions that need to be dealt with. For example, I personally felt a profound sense of abandonment when my father passed away unexpectedly when I was only 16 years old. Although his departure was not intentional, the pain I experienced was both physically and emotionally taxing, affecting me deeply on both internal and external levels.

Other Reasons Why Healing Matters

It's essential to consider other reasons why healing is necessary, including instances of physical, sexual, emotional, verbal, mental, and spiritual abuse. Physical abuse refers to situations where parents, caregivers, teachers, authority figures, partners, spouses, children, or other family members engage in actions such as hitting, beating, pushing, choking, jumping and spitting on, slapping, and tearing down individuals.

Sexual abuse encompasses instances where parents, caregivers, other family members, teachers, authority figures, partners, children, neighbors, friends of the family, bus drivers, janitors, or church members, along with staff, engage in inappropriate sexual behaviors. These behaviors can include touching, groping, licking, kissing, sucking, rubbing, penetrating, raping, exploiting, coercing, threatening, video recording, making victims watch or participate in sexual acts, including pornography, and taking advantage of them.

Mental and psychological abuse involves various harmful actions, such as demeaning, comparing, ignoring, implementing the silent treatment, guilt-tripping, degrading, withholding love, affection, and attention as a form of punishment, lacking love, compliments, words of affirmation, gratitude, and validation during childhood.

Additionally, mental and psychological abuse can entail being disrespected, controlled, mistreated, having power used against the victim, experiencing intimidation, and being demoralized.

It is vital not to overlook the detrimental impact of verbal abuse. Verbal abuse can inflict significant harm and cause deep emotional wounds. Examples of verbal abuse include name calling, cursing, yelling, screaming, and expressing hatred, hurt, anger, and disgust toward an individual. The power of words should never be underestimated, as they can leave lasting scars on a person's self-esteem, welfare, and overall mental health.

Spiritual abuse is a form of manipulation and control that exploits religion, man-made traditions, and psychological strategies to exert power over individuals. It involves making people believe that they are insignificant, doomed to hell, or will face exile unless they conform to the specific expectations and orders of a particular church or religion. This type of abuse can be mainly damaging when it deviates from healthy religious principles and instead serves the personal gain and power of those perpetrating the abuse.

Abuse in any form is deeply traumatizing and leaves lasting wounds. Regardless of the type of trauma one has experienced, healing is essential. Recognizing the need for healing and seeking appropriate support and resources is an important step toward reclaiming one's well-being and moving forward in a healthier and more empowering way.

Finally, it is important to recognize that each of us has caused pain to others. We have been responsible for hurting people, damaging lives, shattering hearts, cheating, rejecting, abandoning, neglecting, lying, stealing, betraying trust, failing to be there for others, being unsupportive, unavailable, and even absent. We need to understand the need for healing that arises from such experiences.

It is important to note that the reasons for needing healing are vast and varied, extending far beyond what was mentioned in the previous paragraphs. Each individual has their own unique experiences, traumas, and challenges that contribute to their need for healing. While it may not be possible to list and articulate every reason for healing, it does not diminish the significance of the healing process. The reality is that there are countless reasons why we need to heal, and each person's journey is personal and multifaceted. It is this recognition of the importance of healing and the willingness to embark on that journey that lays the foundation for growth, resilience, and well-being.

Where to Look for Help with Healing

Drawing from my 26 years of experience in assisting clients with their mental health and life challenges, it is evident that many individuals are unaware that the healing journey begins with acknowledging the need to seek help and engage in open conversations. When faced with a medical health issue, most of us do not hesitate to consult a doctor and share our concerns. The doctor then initiates a treatment plan, starting with identifying the problem from a medical perspective. They may order tests to confirm the diagnosis and proceed to address the issue, sometimes providing a timeline for the healing process.

Similarly, in matters of mental health and emotional well-being, the healing process can begin by recognizing the importance of seeking professional assistance. By engaging in dialogue and sharing one's struggles, individuals can embark on a journey of understanding, self-discovery, and eventual healing. Just as in the medical field, where the doctor plays a crucial role in guiding the treatment process, mental health professionals can provide the necessary support, guidance, and treatment strategies to facilitate healing and promote overall good health.

But unlike the medical field, the process of emotional healing is often complex and not as straightforward. However, the journey toward healing begins with the important step of acknowledging the need to seek help and support. It starts with recognizing that something is amiss emotionally, internally, or mentally.

Please pause for a moment and reflect on the various factors or circumstances that may contribute to your need for healing, and create a comprehensive list of all of your hurts below:

____

____

____

____

____

____

____

____

What are the consequences of you not allowing your emotional wounds and scars to undergo the proper healing process?

____

____

____

____

____

____

____

Before we can embark on the healing process, we must first allow ourselves to truly feel. We need to grant permission to experience our emotions fully. In the next chapter, we will explore the importance of emotions, how to allow ourselves to genuinely feel them, and how to identify our specific emotional states.

Subsequently, we will learn how to navigate and process these emotions effectively. By embarking on this journey, we will enrich our understanding, knowledge, and emotional intelligence, which are significant to the purpose behind writing this book. Most importantly, as we embark on the initial step of embracing our emotions and learning how to feel, we will learn how to heal. I believe suffering starts when we don't allow ourselves to feel. I invite everyone NOT to suffer anymore.

Chapter 3

I Am Scared to Feel!

Are You Afraid to Feel?

I firmly believe that before we can truly embark on the healing process, we must allow ourselves to actually feel. Once we have acknowledged the reasons and the areas requiring healing, I urge you to dig deeper and really experience those emotions. I am asking you to embrace the act of FEELING.

We need to grant ourselves permission to experience our emotions fully. As I frequently tell my clients, *we need to give ourselves permission to feel.*

In this chapter, we will explore the importance of emotions, how to allow ourselves to genuinely feel them, and how to identify our specific emotional states. Later, we will learn how to navigate and process (i.e., deal) these emotions effectively.

In my extensive experience as a psychotherapist, I have come to realize that a significant number of individuals don't like or want to feel. They tend to avoid both experiencing and acknowledging their emotions. Many of us have not been equipped with the tools to properly recognize and understand our feelings, let alone express them or navigate through them effectively. Moreover, we may lack the knowledge and skills to validate, accept, or even simply be present with our emotions. The challenge lies not only in determining what actions to take in response to our emotional experiences but also in first learning how to identify our emotions.

Before we can take action, we must understand the importance of our feelings. It is crucial to value our emotions. We need to shift our beliefs from undervaluing our feelings to recognizing how valuable, precious, and meaningful they are. Before I can try to help change our mindsets of how significant our emotions are, we need to understand why we are apprehensive. In my opinion, one of the reasons is that our emotions are tied to us being vulnerable.

A considerable number of individuals have developed a strong dislike of vulnerability, as we have been conditioned to believe that it signifies weakness. We learned and were taught not to feel – that expressing our emotions and allowing ourselves to be vulnerable was a flaw or a display of being fragile. In particular, men have often been instructed not to embrace their emotions and instead suppress their feelings. On the other hand, women frequently encounter remarks such as "you are too sensitive" or "you are too emotional," further reinforcing the notion that expressing emotions is undesirable. I believe that gender differences and our upbringing significantly influence how both men and women express their feelings, shaping their emotional experiences. For instance, some research indicates that there are noticeable gender differences in the experience and expression of emotions. Various studies and meta-analyses have shown that women and girls are more inclined and permitted to express their emotions compared to men and boys. These differences have been observed in the United States and certain Western European countries. Women tend to display a higher overall level of emotional expression, particularly when it comes to positive emotions and internalizing negative feelings such as sadness and anxiety.[7] Men are more likely to exhibit higher levels of aggression and anger than women, but this may vary depending on the context.

Many of us have witnessed, heard, or experienced these differences. Women and girls are often labeled as "emotional," while men and boys are stereotyped as "action-oriented and doers." Certain girls are taught to disregard their feelings, just like men are told to "ignore

---

[7] Ann M. Kring and Albert H. Gordon, "Sex Differences in Emotion: Expression, Experience, and Physiology," *Journal of Personality and Social Psychology* 74, no. 3 (1998): 668-703.

emotions" or "MAN UP." But what does it truly mean to "MAN UP" or "BE A MAN?" What is society trying to convey to men? And what harmful patterns are they perpetuating? The expectation for boys is to avoid crying, which seems to impact their ability to express their feelings as adults. It is even more disconcerting when individuals are labeled as "crazy" or told that something is wrong with them simply because they are open to their own emotions.

Our upbringing has a major impact on how we view emotions. For instance, a significant number of our parents did not effectively express or openly display their feelings. If they did, it often revolved around only anger or happiness, leaving a limited range of emotional expression. They were not taught that it is acceptable to experience and acknowledge a broad spectrum of emotions. Consequently, many of us have unconsciously adopted this learned behavior, perpetuating the cycle of suppressing or inadequately expressing our feelings, which is a form of learned behavior.

Learned behavior, the acquisition of actions through exposure and experience, is a process where individuals gain knowledge, skills, attitudes, or preferences by interacting with their environment.[8] This behavior, not instinctive but acquired through observation, imitation, instruction, and reinforcement, manifests in various contexts and across different species. For example, a child learns fundamental skills like walking, talking, and using utensils through observation and practice. This is the same when it comes to learning how to feel and why our emotions are important. If our parents didn't model or teach us how to acknowledge our feelings, recognize how important they are, and how to express them, it is completely understandable how many of us don't allow ourselves to feel. Depending on which generation you are from, bottling everything up and keeping everything in is the learned behavior you observed. This isn't a criticism of our parents and other generations before us. It's just an example of how we can't blame ourselves for why we struggle with

[8] "Learned behaviors," Khan Academy, accessed January 2020, https://www.khanac-ademy.org/science/.

our emotions. Our parents did their very best with what they had and what they were taught as well.

It has become apparent that we have not been actively instructed on effectively expressing our emotions and being vulnerable. Despite societal and familial norms and conditioning, I firmly believe (and often share with my clients) that embracing vulnerability is a tremendous source of strength – if we allow ourselves to embrace it. I often say, "Vulnerability is the greatest strength we all can have, especially if we give ourselves permission to be vulnerable." We will look further into vulnerability in the upcoming chapters.

The beauty is we now live in a world that is becoming more receptive to understanding the importance of feeling our emotions. Therapy is more acceptable. As a result, people are becoming aware of how to "unlearn" learned behaviors to help them begin to engage in healthier habits, such as acknowledging that our feelings are important and they matter.

Feelings and Emotions

Having considered the significance of emotions, I think it is an ideal time for us to further explore and understand our feelings and emotions. This exploration can aid us in learning how to feel and identify them.

I believe the definition of feelings and emotions helps us learn how to feel and emote. Feelings refer to the overall state of awareness that exists apart from specific sensations, thoughts, and so on.[9] They encompass emotions, emotional perceptions, attitudes, and the capacity for experiencing and expressing emotions, particularly compassion.

Emotion is a state of consciousness characterized by the experience

---

[9] "Feeling," Dictionary.com, accessed January 2020, https://www.dictionary.com/browse/feeling.

of affective states such as joy, sorrow, fear, hate, or liking.[10] It is distinct from cognitive and volitional states of consciousness. Emotions encompass a range of intense feelings, including agony, betrayal, and any other powerful agitations of the feelings. They are often accompanied by physiological changes like an increased heartbeat or respiration and frequently manifest outwardly through actions like crying or shaking.

If we look at how each word is defined, the definitions provide rich, descriptive explanations that I find fascinating as they contain details often overlooked by many. The words the dictionary uses exemplify how profound our feelings and emotions are, highlighting why we need to allow ourselves to feel.

To better understand our feelings, I would like to explain the different categories of emotions and how they foster a greater capacity for experiencing them. Over the years, I noticed that when helping clients identify their feelings, I had to educate them on the difference between primary and secondary emotions. By doing so, they could grasp each emotion and articulate it by recognizing their depth and character.

According to the APA Dictionary of Psychology, primary emotions encompass a limited range of emotions that are typically universally observed and acknowledged across cultures.[11] It is worth noting that the specific list of primary emotions can vary among different theorists. Examples of primary emotions include contempt, surprise, shame, shyness, and guilt. On the other hand, secondary emotions are emotions that are not universally recognized or exhibited across cultures or emotions that require social experiences to develop. "Mono no aware" is Japanese for the bittersweet awareness of the transient nature of beauty, whereas "Han" in Korea describes a complex feeling of resentment, regret, and unresolved sadness. The

[10] "Emotion," Dictionary.com, accessed January 2020, https://www.dictionary.com/browse/emotion.

[11] "Emotions," APA Dictionary of Psychology, accessed January 2020, http://dictionary.apa.org.

classic example of a secondary emotion is that of schadenfreude – pleasure derived from someone else's misfortune. In America, pride is an example of a secondary emotion, which arises from the combination of primary emotions such as joy and happiness. Other examples of secondary emotions include envy, frustration, and jealousy.

Understanding our emotions can help us feel more comfortable with feeling them. One way of allowing ourselves to feel is to have a better understanding of how to emote them. The word "feeling" can function as a noun, adjective, and verb. For instance, we say, "I feel bad," or express our feelings of sadness and anger. We might convey sentiments like, "I feel like I can't trust you," or more broadly, "I feel like nobody cares." Many individuals have echoed similar statements to themselves, both internally and externally. How many of you have uttered phrases such as "I feel like I lack support," or "I feel like I'm all alone?"

I often advise my clients to refrain from transforming a feeling into a statement or a belief. When we express our emotions, it is important to articulate an actual feeling rather than a mere statement. Let's take the example from above, "I feel like I lack support." I lack support isn't a feeling or emotion. That is a statement. How do you feel about lacking support? "I feel sad because I lack support" is identifying the feeling. Or take the remark, "I feel like no one cares." What is the feeling? There isn't a feeling because it's being implied instead of explicitly stated. We can learn how to express our feelings directly by being assertive and direct about how we actually feel. We can say, "I am hurt because it seems no one cares, or I feel hurt because no one cares." Acknowledging that you are experiencing hurt rather than making a conclusive statement is crucial to understanding. By allowing yourself to say I am hurt because no one cares or I feel hurt because no one cares helps the individual to become vulnerable and connected to his or her feelings. It allows you to really be present with your emotions about the situation you are experiencing, allowing you to now express that emotion instead of keeping it in. It helps you to accomplish your goal of learning how to allow yourself to feel and literally identify specific emotions.

Similarly, "I feel disappointed because I am all alone" is better than "I feel like I am all alone." In order for us to learn how to deal and heal we must encourage ourselves to actually articulate the actual feelings we are experiencing. We need to pay attention to our emotional reactions and responses. We need to say the feeling.

I invite you to take a moment and give it a try. Recall a feeling you experienced this morning, any kind of change. Anything, and jot it down:

____

____

____

____

____

____

Is that an actual feeling? Did you utilize the feeling as a verb, noun, or adjective? What is your emotional reaction and response? Were you able to genuinely express the emotion? If so, that's great. If not, let's give it another try. Let's consider a time when you experienced a range of emotions. Reflect on a moment when you felt a shift in your emotional state. Go ahead and write it down below.

____

____

____

____

____

____

For those of you who find writing down your feelings challenging, that's completely understandable. What I am strongly encouraging you not to do is write down "I feel like…". Please try to write down the actual emotion you are feeling. I listed examples of primary and secondary emotions earlier to help those readers who find it difficult to identify their feelings. Many people find it difficult to tap into their emotional side, but connecting to your emotions is essential.

Exploring Emotional Intelligence

We often question why some individuals, both men and women, struggle with emotional intelligence. As defined by the APA Dictionary of Psychology, emotional intelligence involves the capacity and ability to process emotional information and utilize it in cognitive activities and reasoning.[12] This concept was introduced by American psychologists Peter Salovey and John D. Mayer. According to Mayer and Salovey's 1997 model, emotional intelligence consists of four abilities: accurately perceiving and evaluating emotions, accessing and eliciting to enhance thinking, understanding emotional language and utilizing emotional information, and regulating one's own and others' emotions to foster personal growth and well-being. These ideas gained popularity through the widely acclaimed book *Emotional Intelligence*, written by American psychologist and science journalist Daniel J. Goleman, who also expanded the definition to encompass various personality variables.[13]

In what way can individuals develop emotional intelligence when they frequently receive messages such as "don't feel," "move on," "suck it up," "solve the issue," or "get over it"? The answer is we can begin to deprogram our brains by first recognizing the significance of our feelings, then start to reframe our negative thoughts about our emotions by saying it is okay to feel and connect with my emotions,

---

[12] "Emotional Intelligence," APA Dictionary of Psychology, accessed January 2020, http://dictionary.apa.org.

[13] Daniel J. Goleman, *Emotional Intelligence*, 10th Anniversary Edition (New York: Bantam Books, 1994).

and finally begin to identify what we are actually feeling by expressing those emotions not only to ourselves also to others. We can relearn and obtain emotional intelligence by understanding how we interpret and assess our emotions precisely, how we verbalize and express them when they are connected to our thoughts, our ability to understand our emotions as well as others, and how we control and manage them.

Even though many individuals struggle with emotional intelligence and accepting and openly expressing their feelings, it is widely acknowledged that our emotions are inherent and natural. Regardless of how diligently we attempt to disregard, ignore, deny, overlook, repress, or suppress them, **THOSE FEELINGS** are still there. It is challenging for someone to be evaluated based on their emotional state when they have been taught to disregard and suppress their feelings. But the feelings are there, and they persist.

You know that persistent, nagging feeling– it's elusive, hard to define, yet unmistakably there, indicating that something isn't quite right. Sometimes, it takes a while for us to comprehend and fully grasp it. However, by understanding the vital importance of our emotions, I strongly believe we can allow and grant ourselves permission to acknowledge and express our feelings. *We can empower ourselves to recognize and articulate our emotions.*

Why It Matters

I provide a disclaimer to ALL of my clients. If you choose to work with me, be prepared to experience discomfort because I will encourage you to truly FEEL and identify your emotions. I will ask you probing questions such as "How do you feel?" What does that feeling feel like?" "What emotions are arising within you at this moment?" "How did you express your feelings?" "Did others understand your emotional state?" and "How did you handle your emotions?"

What I don't ask is, "How does that make you feel?" According to reality therapy, nothing external has the power to compel us to feel or act in a certain way unless we willingly choose to do so.[14] If we attribute our emotions to external factors, we inadvertently give them control over our feelings (i.e., "They made us do it"). But not doing so means that we take back control, which also involves being accountable for them, and therefore, vulnerable.

I strongly encourage you to embrace vulnerability. Let go of any preconceived notions that associate feelings and vulnerability with weakness. Our emotions hold immense significance for every human being. They serve as reminders of our authenticity, connection to reality, and distinctiveness from robots or machines. We are not MACHINES. We do not have an on and off button. Emotions remind us that we are humans. They serve as exceptional teachers, reminding us of our inherent worth and reinforcing our sense of self-value. We matter, and our presence holds significance. We are important, cherished, and seen.

Many of us suffer and grapple with a sense of invisibility, feeling unnoticed and disregarded. I urge you to vocalize this affirmation: "I **and my feelings do matter**." It is critical to express and share your feelings, acknowledge your thoughts, verbalize them, identify what matters and what holds significance, and recognize them all. Your feelings are an integral part of who you are.

How to Acknowledge Your Feelings

I understand that many of you are pondering an important question: HOW? How do we engage in this transformative work? And how does this relate to the healing process?

In my view, allowing ourselves to feel is intricately intertwined with the healing journey. How can one heal from anything if we don't even know what we are feeling, let alone how to navigate and address those emotions to facilitate healing? We all need to learn how to deal with our feelings to help them to heal.

---

[14] William Glasser, Counseling with Choice Theory: The New Reality Therapy, (New York: Harper Perennial, 2000).

To initiate the healing process, it is vital to genuinely experience the emotions associated with pain, hurt, disappointment, and anguish. Reflect on that injury, that hurt, that disappointment, that break-up, that death, that loss, that...

____ .

Fill in the blank of your experience.

Take a breath and allow yourself to think about that pain, wound, distress, injury, or trauma you experienced. What is it? What transpired? What didn't occur as you had hoped?

Whatever you envisioned or recalled, how are you feeling? How did you feel at that moment or when it happened? Can you express and verbalize that emotion? I acknowledge that this is challenging, but I encourage you to experience it fully. It is okay to connect with your emotions and be vulnerable.

Once you permit yourself to feel, take a moment to recognize those emotions. Familiarize yourself with their sensations. Feel and experience that pain, sadness, guilt, shame, embarrassment, disappointment, anxiety, fear, loneliness, agony, despair, discouragement, loss of control, feeling lost, and any of the other diverse emotions you have encountered that I may not have explicitly mentioned.

All of us need to acquire the knowledge and capacity to confront, acknowledge, and manage our emotions, thoughts, and the events associated with them. When I refer to events, I mean the situations, incidents, and occurrences that take place in our lives and have had or continue to have a significant impact on us. We have thoughts, emotions, and reactions to these events, and we need to know how important it is to learn how to effectively deal with them.

No matter what you were taught, our feelings are important. We have to FEEL, and not just GET OVER IT.

Chapter 4

What Do You Mean by DEAL?

Why Dealing With Your Feelings Matters

I encourage everyone to deal with trauma, but how? In my work with clients, I actively promote a process of addressing and confronting their wounds. This approach assists them in navigating through experiences of trauma, pain, sorrow, and emotional distress. I urge each individual to recognize the source of their pain and its associated emotions. Following this, I encourage them to explore their response to their hurt, the factors contributing to it, and how they were affected.

In the preceding chapters, I encouraged each of you to document all the instances in which you experienced emotional pain. If you haven't done so yet, please make a comprehensive list of all your hurts below. I understand this can be challenging, but it is an essential step for unfolding the ongoing healing process.

____

____

____

____

____

____

____

____

Now, let's identify the individuals who have caused you harm and examine the ways in which they have inflicted that hurt upon you.

Engaging in this exercise marks the beginning of the second step towards healing, which is to deal. I strongly encourage you to confront hurt by acknowledging its presence and actively processing it. This same process applies to dealing with grief, pain, heartache, abandonment, and any other challenges, hardships, tragedies, or struggles that you may be facing or have experienced.

When I emphasize the significance of dealing with their emotional wounds, my clients often react with questions like, "What does she mean by deal? Deal with what exactly? How should I deal with it? When and where should I start? What does the process entail?" After a brief moment, some even go back to saying, "I'm over it" or "I've moved on" or "I've let it go" or even "I just ignore it."

Do these statements and questions ring a bell? They mean that it's now time to deal with your pain.

Breaking Down How To Deal

The primary objective of dealing is to address, face, and confront your feelings. This involves facing your emotions, the events, the situations, the problems, or the issues at hand and giving them the validation they deserve. As we will explore deeper in the next chapter, validation is an incredibly potent coping mechanism. But before we delve into that, I want to encourage each of you to initiate the healing journey by reflecting on the pain, embracing it, and openly discussing it.

There are various avenues through which we can facilitate this. One option is to converse with a therapist or counselor, sharing your disappointments and concerns. Another approach could involve journaling or expressing your hurt through creative outlets such as poetry, song lyrics, or writing a book. It can be beneficial and healthy for us all to make our experiences tangible by simply speaking and telling our truth about the matter, fully recognizing and acknowledging it.

Consider how Sarah confronted her feelings. I requested that she share her thoughts and emotions regarding her mother's failure to express pride in her or tell her she is proud of her. She instantly experienced a surge of hurt, disappointment, and pain. She appeared shocked and taken aback by the intensity of her emotional reaction and the response evoked by my question. Restlessly shifting in her chair, she became fidgety. Then, out poured some remarkable disclosures. "Do you know that even to this day, I still yearn for her approval?" Tears streamed down her face as she continued, "Throughout my life, I have been waiting for my mother to utter those simple words to me. I just want to hear her say 'good job' and 'I am proud of you.' Is that too much to ask? Is it so difficult?" When Sarah attempted to express herself to her mother, she would dismissively respond, "What are you talking about, girl? There you go again." Her mother's reaction only reignited the pain of disappointment, causing Sarah to exclaim, "Damn Mama."

Unbeknownst to Sarah, she needed to confront and address this lingering pain from the past by feeling and dealing with it in the present. Going beyond merely identifying her emotions by talking about them is one way of tackling difficult feelings. After multiple therapy sessions where she explored her feelings in a safe space, she gradually began to experience improvement and healing from her mother's limitations. Sarah started to take pride in herself, beginning to be proud and accept when others expressed how proud they were of her. She ceased disregarding their compliments and started embracing them. This marked a significant accomplishment and a notable shift in her mood, behavior, beliefs, and thoughts, all becoming more optimistic.

In the end, Sarah changed her mindset, letting go of the belief that her mother's approval was the sole measure of importance. It became clear to her that compliments hold significance and are essential, regardless of who says or delivers them. It was a transformative journey for Sarah, highlighting the importance of understanding that compliments are valuable and necessary, regardless of the source.

Through my practice with clients, I have identified three effective methods for dealing with healing: taking the time to sit with our emotions, acknowledging and validating them, and engaging in a thoughtful process of introspection and growth. In other words, sit, validate, and process. I want to discuss the first of these in this chapter – how to sit with your emotions.

Sitting with Yourself

When I suggest "SIT," I'm encouraging you to actively sit with yourself, embracing your thoughts, feelings, and the situation at hand. It's a plea to acknowledge, recognize, and establish a deeper connection with your inner self. It's not merely identifying your emotions but initiating a process of making peace with them. There is an old saying – "peace be still," – which implies that tranquility can be attained when we grant ourselves the space to sit and be still.

What does the phrase "peace be still" evoke in your mind? What's the first automatic thought that comes to mind?

Automatic thoughts are a term commonly used in Cognitive Behavior Therapy (CBT) to describe thoughts that arise instantly and spontaneously when encountering specific situations. According to the APA Dictionary of Psychology, automatic thoughts refer to, "thoughts that are instantaneous, habitual, and non-conscious. Automatic thoughts affect a person's mood and actions. Thoughts that have been learned and habitually repeated that they occur without cognitive effort."[15]

Automatic thoughts are thoughts that come instantly regardless of the trigger and the event. They are rapid and constant without any effort on your part. To identify your automatic thoughts, it can be helpful to write down what you are saying to yourself or thinking immediately in response to a particular situation. You can gain insight into your automatic thoughts and thinking patterns by tracking and recording your thoughts. Now, take a moment to jot down your initial thoughts when you hear the phrase "PEACE BE STILL."

____

____

____

____

____

____

It is crucial for us to start recognizing our automatic thoughts. This is an important step towards understanding ourselves better and learning how to be comfortable with our thoughts by sitting with our emotions.

[15] "Automatic Thoughts," APA Dictionary of Psychology, accessed January 2020, http://dictionary.apa.org.

In CBT, Dr. Aaron Beck developed a tool called a thought record to assist individuals in recognizing their automatic thoughts and comprehending the sudden shifts in mood and behavior. I have adapted this technique to accommodate those who may be opposed to recording their thoughts or find it challenging to write them down. Instead, I encourage clients to embrace the practice of sitting with their thoughts and actively identifying and recognizing their automatic thoughts. Embracing this process of self-reflection and stillness can be immensely valuable.

Similar to my client Sarah, who learned how to sit still, encounter, and address her emotions, your reactions may echo hers. Many of her responses included phrases like, "Do I really have to stay and be still? Are you suggesting I shouldn't move?" Although being still might help, what I'm truly saying is be fully present with yourself and be present in this very moment. Be silent, quiet, and attuned to your thoughts. I frequently find myself saying things like, "Stay grounded and not wander off. Take it slow and slow down." In saying this, I'm trying to emphasize that finding peace involves learning the art of being still and truly embracing the essence of stillness. By being quiet, sitting down, and remaining in a single place, you foster a sense of unity within yourself by being one with yourself. This first practice of dealing with our emotions enables individuals to recognize, acknowledge, delve into, and explore how a particular event has impacted them. It provides an opportunity for honesty, transparency, and, hopefully, a willingness to be vulnerable with oneself.

Sitting with the pain, hurt, disappointment, and trauma is an essential step toward initiating the healing process. That's because when we sit, we embrace being fully present and hinder and prevent tendencies such as avoidance, denial, escapism, numbness, and self-deception.

Self-deception

Each of us carries within us false truths – in other words, the lies that we tell ourselves. Phrases like "I don't care," "No one cares," "It's not important," "It's no big deal," or "It doesn't matter" may have echoed in our heads or even been spoken aloud. I confess that I've caught myself uttering these statements, and many of my clients have admitted to doing the same. Unfortunately, we often use these declarations precisely when the problem, person, or situation does matter. You are significant, important, and deserving of care and attention, even if we attempt to convince ourselves otherwise.

Sitting with your emotions conveys a different message. It says, "Your feelings are a big deal. They are important. You do matter. People care about you."

I believe false truths create what I refer to as "self-imprisonment." We become trapped in our own lies, unknowingly restricting ourselves and placing limitations on our lives and relationships. We subconsciously confine ourselves to a metaphorical prison where we put ourselves in a box, depriving ourselves of freedom. Our freedom is derived from embracing radical honesty and transparency. Through honesty, we grant our permission to speak and acknowledge our TRUTHS. It is important to note that knowing our truths is different from speaking them. Both can be challenging. The former is what happens when you identify your feelings, but the latter takes you to the next phase of dealing.

I often encourage people at this stage of their healing journey to "live in their truth." Once you have discovered your truth – the emotions you are feeling – you can begin to gain clarity about your own reality – the emotions you are living through. The beauty of living your truth lies in the fact that you will no longer say, "I don't know what's wrong" or "I don't know how I feel." Instead, we can consciously operate from the truth, even when it may be painful, hurtful, challenging, self-centered, frightening, or goes against what others expect of us (what we are SUPPOSED to do).

Living our truth also reveals that we all possess truths that empower us to embrace our authentic selves. We hold the power to escape the emotional jail we are in and experience freedom – to step beyond the confines of our self-imposed prison and break free from the limitations and restrictions we have placed upon ourselves. We embark on a transformative journey by granting ourselves permission not just to identify but to express our truths, even when it feels uncomfortable within.

It's time to let go of false truths, lies, and dishonesty. Instead, we must learn to be still and sit with our truths, our emotions, our pain, and our discomfort – even when it feels agonizing and uncertain. I implore you to actively sit with your emotions, as it can be a beautiful process if you allow yourself to be vulnerable.

Take a moment and affirm to yourself, "What is my truth? No more lies. What am I genuinely feeling and thinking about right now?"

____

____

____

____

____

____

____

____

Learning how to emote, experience, and express your emotions is crucial. Emoting involves understanding and acknowledging our feelings and allowing ourselves to sit and be still with the feelings we have uncovered and experienced. It means being fully present, transparent, attuned, intentional, and purposeful with ourselves. While we often find it natural to offer advice and solve other people's problems, we tend to avoid addressing our own issues and run away from ourselves. By sitting with our emotions, we can begin the process of self-reflection by confronting and dealing with our truths, rather than avoiding, attempting to "move on," "get over it," or just plain ignoring them.

I want to emphasize that many of us have unresolved issues that we tend to avoid by running from our feelings. I urge you instead, as part of learning to deal with your emotions, to grant yourself permission to confront them by first sitting with them.

Chapter 5

What Do You Mean by DEAL Through Validation?

What Do You Mean by Validation?

ONE of the most effective approaches to healing, that I find beneficial, is validation. Webster's Dictionary defines validation as "recognition or affirmation that a person or their feelings or opinions are valid or worthwhile."[16] Research and studies have consistently demonstrated that validation plays a pivotal role in shaping our sense of self, self-worth, core beliefs, and self-esteem.

Understanding that our existence and experiences hold value is crucial during our childhood. We need to understand that our feelings are important. This process begins in our earliest years, from the moment we are born, as we rely on parents, caregivers, and guardians to let us know that we are important and that our feelings matter. Our mere existence and very being gains validation through words, interactions, acknowledgments, treatment, verbal and nonverbal cues, emotional availability, and support (or lack thereof) from our parents, caretakers, and guardians.

The circle of individuals involved in validating us extends to teachers, pastors, relatives, and close friends – any and all significant figures in a child's life who profoundly impact how we perceive the world and how we were brought up. They have influenced our lives in deep ways and continue to do so. We learn the art of validation by observing and internalizing the behaviors of those who have validated us in the past.

[16] "Validation," Merriam-Webster.com, accessed January 2020, https://www.merri-am-webster.com/dictionary/validation.

Validation is not only essential during our formative years but remains a vital aspect of our emotional well-being throughout our lives. I often emphasize the necessity of learning how to validate our own existence, particularly when we may not have received enough of it during our childhood. Recognizing the importance of validation and actively incorporating it into our interactions can contribute significantly to our healing and personal growth – learning how to deal with our emotions and not just feel them.

During our formative years, we receive validation through a myriad of avenues from our parents, including their emotional intelligence, behaviors, gestures, undertones, and reactions. All of these elements collectively contribute to shaping our understanding of our self-worth and our place in the world. As responsible adults, we have the opportunity and responsibility to recognize the significance of validation and ensure that we create an environment where our children feel seen, heard, valued, and enough. Through this nurturing process, we pave the way for their emotional well-being and growth. For those of you who are parents or aspire to become parents, you play a vital role in nurturing feelings of love, recognition, acknowledgment, and self-worth in your children through the powerful concept of validation.

Please pause for a moment and take some time to contemplate and introspect about your emotional, mental, and physical needs during your childhood. **Were these needs adequately fulfilled?**

Reflect on aspects of your childhood and how they might have influenced your emotional development. During your upbringing, did you ever witness or experience instances where your parents seemed to ignore you, utilize the silent treatment, overlook your presence, or make you feel invisible? Did you sense that you needed to be either perfect or troublesome to gain their attention?

Moreover, did you feel genuinely cared for? Were your parents expressive of their pride in you (i.e., proud of you), and did they remember to communicate this to you? Or did they dismiss your feelings when you encountered painful, embarrassing, sad, or hurtful incidents, simply instructing you to "get over them?" Were you hugged and reassured of your parents' affectionate feelings towards you, or were your feelings neglected and not physically reaffirmed?

Take a moment to recall a specific instance from your childhood where you faced an issue – any problem you can remember. *Take your time and concentrate on that particular moment.*

Try to recollect your parent, caregiver, teacher, pastor, or close relative when you confide in them about the issue. Did they tend to your needs? Did they take care of it, listen, reassure you that it will be okay? How did they support you? Did they listen to you and provide reassurance that everything would be alright? How did they offer their support? Did they choose to guide you on how to handle the situation, or did they take direct action to resolve it, depending on what the issue was? Or did they seem to ignore the problem, remain silent, or make you feel responsible, blaming you for what happened? Your answers to these questions will help you better understand different examples of validation, especially during your childhood experiences.

Digging Deeper into Validation

To illustrate the concept of validation, let me share the experience of my client, Maria. Throughout our sessions, we explored her emotional journey, and it became evident that she craved significant attention and validation from others. Specifically, she sought validation from men and colleagues at her workplace and even relied on material possessions to boost her self-esteem. As we explored her past, she identified a lack of attention and external validation from her family.

During one of our sessions, Maria opened up about her struggles with feeling unloved by her husband and people in general. She expressed a constant sense of needing to do, be, or provide something to gain love and recognition from others, feeling as though she needed to prove her importance constantly. Maria referred to herself as a "people pleaser," believing that she must always be there for everyone because it's the right thing to do and that they depend on her.

As our sessions continued, Maria gradually began to open up more, and she shared the deep unhappiness she was experiencing. She described a persistent feeling of emptiness and a sense of inadequacy. She revealed how unhappy she was and expressed feeling lonely, empty, and not good enough.

I took a moment to genuinely acknowledge Maria's feelings and thoughts of inadequacy, unlovability, emptiness, and unhappiness. I assured her that it was okay to express these emotions and encouraged her to share why she was experiencing such feelings. As our conversation unfolded, she began to talk about her relationship with her husband, explaining that she often felt unwanted, unloved, and unimportant despite her efforts to meet his needs and make him happy. Curious about the depth of these feelings, I asked if she had encountered similar emotions in the past. Maria responded candidly, revealing that she had been grappling with these feelings her entire life.

Maria's actions of not just identifying her emotions but actively experiencing them was genuinely impressive. I offered her words of praise, complimenting and acknowledging her courage in opening up about such challenging experiences. I validated the importance of identifying and speaking the truth of the emotional burden she was carrying. By offering empathy and understanding, I hoped to create a safe space for Maria to continue on the journey of dealing with her emotions and move toward healing.

After she expressed her gratitude, I gently urged Maria to delve deeper into the origins of her feelings of hurt, disappointment, and sadness linked to her sense of being unimportant, empty, and unloved. As she opened up further, she revealed that her father had not been a consistent presence throughout her life, often coming in and out. Meanwhile, her mother won custody and was responsible for raising Maria and her brother. However, despite being physically present, her mother was constantly preoccupied and rarely made time to see her, let alone attend to her needs. Through this revelation, Maria unveiled a poignant history of feeling abandoned by her father and emotionally neglected by her mother. This emotional void left her grappling with profound feelings of inadequacy, emptiness, and a deep yearning for love and importance.

I offered Maria my understanding and compassion, recognizing the immense impact of her early experiences on her current emotional state. By acknowledging her pain and validating her emotions, I aimed to create an environment of trust and support, allowing her to confront these deeply rooted issues.

She vividly recounted a painful chapter from her past, a time when she faced relentless bullying at school. When she mustered the courage to confide in her mother about the ordeal, she received a disheartening response: "What did you do to provoke the girls?" Her mother's response left her feeling blamed and unsupported. Seeking solace from her father, she was met with the repeated phrase, "Baby, give me a minute. Daddy is busy," leaving her feeling dismissed and unheard. Turning to her brother for help was no better. She was met with silence and inaction, deepening her sense of abandonment. The fact that Maria and her brother attended the same school added to her feeling of being let down.

In the absence of parental and sibling support, she made a pivotal decision. She believed that if she acted kind and accommodating towards the mean group of kids – "her bullies" – they might stop tormenting her. She internalized the belief that she had to take matters into her own hands because her mother, father, and brother seemed indifferent to her struggles. She started to think that if she pleased everyone, they would love her.

Unfortunately, this mindset of constantly seeking approval seeped into every aspect of her life. It affected her ability to set boundaries and made her reliant on hearing compliments, accolades, and expressions of love from others in order to feel worthwhile, loved, important, and good enough. She felt inadequate and believed nothing she did was ever enough, especially in her own eyes. This belief led her to prioritize others over herself, always putting their needs ahead of her own. Putting others first and neglecting herself became a learned behavior.

These deep-rooted patterns of seeking external validation and neglecting her own well-being became ingrained and persisted across various areas of her life. It became apparent that understanding and addressing these underlying issues would be essential for her growth and healing. Only through exploring these complex emotions could she work toward reclaiming her sense of self-worth and identity.

Maria's story sheds light on how many of us experienced a lack of validation during our formative and instrumental years, thereby never forming the resources to validate ourselves and always seeking external validation. It's essential to recognize and articulate these experiences, as they can profoundly impact our emotional development and well-being. By acknowledging these struggles, we can gain a deeper understanding of how validation (or the absence of it) is crucial for developing feelings that we are important. Learning how to validate our own emotions teaches us that our feelings matter, shapes our beliefs and behaviors as adults, and moves us closer to begin working toward healing and growth.

The Importance of Validating Ourselves

The lack of support, meeting our needs, and validation from our parents, caregivers, and guardians can be attributed to various reasons, including their limited emotional intelligence. As discussed in Chapter 3, emotional intelligence involves our ability to recognize, express, and verbalize our feelings as well as our capacity to understand and empathize with the emotions of others. We learn to navigate our emotions by observing how our parents, caregivers, guardians, teachers, and other close adults express and respond to their own feelings and ours when we were young.

During this crucial developmental stage, we were exposed to a range of emotions such as sadness, hurt, fear, shame, defeat, annoyance, uncertainty, discouragement, and disappointment. Our guardians served as models, teaching us whether it was acceptable to experience emotions, express them openly, be vulnerable, seek healthy ways to cope with our emotions, respond to others' feelings, and validate our emotional experiences. Its absence in our parental figures may have impacted our own emotional development and ability to navigate the complexities of our feelings.

During our developmental years, it was of immense significance that our feelings, our existence, personalities, achievements, and accomplishments were all seen, validated, recognized, acknowledged, understood, and empathized with. Each aspect of ourselves mattered and was important and meaningful. And if that was missing, we lacked a key need: validation.

Even as adults, we often confront a lack of validation. When you engage in conversations with a parent, you may find yourself yearning for their approval, reassurance, and the ability to make you feel worthy, "good enough," and valued. It's common for individuals to believe that receiving these from their parent (or anyone else) will alleviate the feelings of inadequacy or sense of being uncared for. However, when these expectations aren't met, many of us end up feeling even worse. Even if you receive validation, some may still experience a lingering sense that something is missing or an insatiable need for more and more approval.

Validation assumes a paramount role in dealing with these emotional hurts, as it profoundly aids individuals in the healing journey to cope with various challenges. In the absence of (or inadequate) external validation, it is our responsibility to learn to validate ourselves. Here's how to do it.

As mentioned in the previous chapter, I encouraged you to reflect on any hurt, issue, or trauma that may have been overlooked or disregarded by your parents or caregivers.

Take a moment to pause and reflect on this. If it helps, gently close your eyes. Now, open your eyes and jot down your emotions.

What do you feel?

____

____

____

____

____

____

____

____

After recognizing and putting those feelings into words, it's time to acknowledge them. Speak to yourself and affirm, "I am hurt because..." and complete the statement with a candid expression of your emotions:

I am hurt because ____

____

____

____

____ .

It is crucial to grasp the significance of these feelings, allowing yourself to understand that it's completely okay to experience them. Show empathy towards yourself and acknowledge why the hurt persists. Take a few more moments to fully engage your senses. **Notice** them. Be present in the moment and attune yourself to each sensation. Sit with them. Allow yourself to express how challenging this process may be while also recognizing the importance of confronting these experiences. Remind yourself that you have every right to feel your emotions and whatever happened to you was undoubtedly hurtful. Now validate your own experience. Be kind to yourself and give yourself what you need right now. Take a step towards self-validation and acknowledge your experience, feelings, and most importantly, your existence.

Chapter 6

What Do You Mean DEAL Through Processing?

Who Needs to Process?

PROCESSING is a fundamental skill that each individual must practice. According to the New Oxford American Dictionary, processing involves performing a series of mechanical or chemical operations on something with the intention of altering or preserving it.[17] In cognitive terms, processing encompasses a wide range of mental functions, including acquiring, storing, interpreting, manipulating, transforming, and utilizing knowledge. These activities involve essential functions like attention, perception, learning, and problem-solving. In this context, "processing" goes beyond simply updating and reexamining old memories and emotions. It involves developing a new language to describe, experience, and understand our past and present experiences.

Learning how to process is of utmost importance in the therapeutic world. Regardless of the specific therapeutic modality a therapist employs, every clinician, psychiatrist, psychiatric nurse, or behavioral health staff will ask individuals receiving mental health treatment to engage in the PROCESS of healing. The significance of processing is such that mental health programs often have dedicated "processing groups" to facilitate this essential aspect of the healing journey.

When it comes to dealing with our emotions, I strongly encourage all of us to learn and implement processing. Understanding, comprehending, and coming to terms with our past hurts and present

17 "Processing," New Oxford American Dictionary, Oxford University Press, 2023.

challenges is essential to initiating the healing process. But beyond merely sitting with our emotions and validating them, we must actively engage in processing our feelings, thoughts, events, problems, wounds, betrayals, and pain that have shaped our experiences.

It's important to note that processing your issues without the guidance of a therapist can be more challenging. However, there are coping mechanisms and interventions I have implemented to help my clients process their wounds and hurt outside of therapy.

The Raw Letter

One technique for processing involves crafting a raw letter, a profound and cathartic expression of thoughts and emotions. It is a heartfelt and unfiltered message addressed directly to the person responsible for the pain and issues you are experiencing. The purpose is to courageously share your deepest, darkest, and most authentic thoughts, laying bare your subconscious fears and vulnerabilities. This letter serves as a means to be transparent about your truth, speaking directly to the individual who triggered these emotions and describing their experiences and memories.

I encourage you to consider writing a raw letter to different recipients, depending on the situation. This might include writing a letter to the person who caused the hurt and pain, to the abuser, to the rapist, or to the person who abandoned you. The recipients of the raw letter could be yourself, your mother, father, grandparents, uncles, aunts, teachers, current or former romantic partners, spouses, pastors, siblings, cousins, friends or ex-friends, bosses, or even co-workers. Essentially, the letter is addressed to anyone who elicited unwanted and hurtful emotions within you.

Through this profound act of self-expression, the raw letter can help you bear your soul, offering a pathway to release and understanding. By writing to the person or persons who played a role in your emotional struggles, you can explore and express your innermost thoughts and feelings, thus confronting and dealing with your emotions and putting you on the path of eventual healing and growth.

This exercise grants individuals the remarkable opportunity to access, reveal, uncover, and explore a part of their minds and psyche that may have remained dormant, repressed, ignored, or expressed in harmful ways. The raw letter is an intervention that empowers us, providing a voice for our unheard stories, revealing our secrets, illuminating our darkness, and unveiling unseen aspects of ourselves. Moreover, it allows us to verbalize feelings and thoughts we may have kept inside, dismissing their importance as if they didn't matter.

Through this exercise, we can freely express all our emotions and experiences on paper, directed towards the particular person who played a role in our struggles. The beauty of this process lies in the absence of judgment, consequences, or backlash. We have the freedom to be vulnerable, transparent, and utterly honest, without overthinking or holding back.

Nevertheless, I must emphasize a caveat: This exercise can be highly emotional, frightening, and draining. The safe part of this assignment is that no one will see the letter. This letter will **NEVER** be given to its intended recipient; it is a strictly private exercise. Not sharing this letter allows you the freedom to express everything and permits you to release your emotions on the page without reservation.

I encourage you to take your time with the raw letter. The length can vary from just one or two paragraphs to 20 pages or more, depending on how much you need to release, let go, and express yourself or that particular person (who will never see it).

If you find that you are confronting heavy emotions as you write, I encourage you not to rush the process; keep writing. There may be more to say, and that's perfectly okay. This raw letter can take various amounts of time to complete – minutes to hours, days to weeks, or even months. The duration depends on various reasons, such as the person to whom the letter is written, the complexity of the events that transpired, and, most importantly, how you feel. It correlates with the depth of the trauma, hurt, pain, and wounds you're dealing with and the extent of the healing required.

This letter is a powerful means of catharsis, where you can unleash your resentment, anger, hurt, love, hatred, disappointment, yearnings, needs, desires, wants, agony, shame, embarrassment, wishes, fears, and dreams. Feel free to use colorful language to express yourself fully; don't hold back. Take your time. This is a personal process exclusively for you, and there's no need to overthink it. Just let it ALL OUT.

It is essential to understand that writing this raw letter does not cause harm to anyone, and no one can hurt you in this vulnerable state. This exercise provides a safe space to confront and process emotions and experiences without fear of repercussion, ultimately facilitating healing and growth.

This raw letter serves as a valuable tool for processing your feelings, thoughts, events, and behaviors. It provides an opportunity to reveal your truths and articulate things you may believe you'd never say or express. It offers a way to release the burden of carrying emotional baggage that you've been lugging around for your entire life. Most importantly, it allows you to do so without fear of judgment, ridicule, or criticism of **your truth**.

As you write the raw letter, take note of the emotions that arise in the process. Identify how you feel as you write each word and recognize your feelings after you've finished writing it. As you reread the raw letter, observe how you're feeling. It's essential to validate these emotions. They are valid and a reflection of your innermost self.

Acknowledging your emotions is essential. The letter is an opportunity to experience emotions along with reliving them. Let those tears flow if you feel them. Allow the anger to come out, along with the sadness, resentment, and neglect you've experienced. It's essential to express how their absence affected you and how you've struggled with feelings of inadequacy and not feeling good enough. You can vent your feelings, asking questions like, *"DADDY, why couldn't you love me? What did I do so wrong?"* and expressing *your frustrations by screaming, "Mama, why did you put that man in front of me? Why did you take his side?"* You can address your grandmother, *"Grandma, why did you keep telling me I will never be anything just like my mom and dad? Why couldn't you see I wasn't them?"*

In most cases, people experience a profound sense of relief after completing this exercise. A feeling of lightness and liberation often washes over you. If you feel that sense of relief, it signifies that you've done an excellent job of processing your emotions and bringing them to the surface.

One thing that repeatedly comes to the forefront when writing a raw letter is acknowledging the necessity to grieve the desired connection that they might never experience or have with the person they are writing the letter to, mourning the potential unmet desires, and recognizing the absence of the relationship that they never had. This process of grieving is relevant for adult children who have fractured or broken relationships with their parents, grandparents, or caregivers. It's also relevant for adults grieving other relationships that are lacking.

The use of the raw letter aids in navigating these complex emotions and thoughts. It becomes a means to address the grieving process associated with the loss of the desired relationship that the individual deeply longs and yearns for. By writing a raw letter, individuals can mourn the absence of what they never had or might never have. This paves the way for accepting their current reality and creating space to potentially improve their present relationship.

Remember, this exercise is for you and you alone. Embrace the opportunity to unburden yourself, confront your emotions and the person you are writing to, and find solace in the act of releasing them. Allow this raw letter to be a powerful tool in your journey of self-discovery and healing.

Our total self is composed of many intricate parts, some of which we might not even acknowledge, recognize, or be aware of their existence. Each part of ourselves deserves an outlet – a chance to be heard and seen. Every aspect of our being matters and holds significance. The raw letter serves as a powerful tool to tap into every part of ourselves. It provides an excellent avenue for exploration, free from any filters or inhibitions, offering candid expression and allowing us to embrace and address each part of our identity.

Therefore, embrace the journey of self-discovery that the raw letter offers. Allow yourself to unravel the various layers of your emotions and experiences. Give each part of your being the opportunity to find its voice and let yourself shine through. The raw letter is a safe and liberating space for you to delve into the depths of your soul and embrace your authentic self.

What Comes After the Raw Letter

Once you are done with the raw letter, you aren't done with the process. After you've finished pouring your emotions onto the pages in this raw letter, you're presented with a range of options for what to do with it. Although the completion of it may have brought you some relief, it's essential for you to consider what steps you want to take next. Here are some options:

1. **Write an actual letter to the person that is different from your raw letter:** It can be a heartfelt expression of your feelings directly to the individual you are addressing in the raw letter. This can be a way to communicate your emotions and potentially start a dialogue.

2. **Create a template for discussion:** If you don't feel comfortable giving them a letter or if the situation requires a more in-person approach, you can write a template outlining the key points and topics you want to discuss. This can serve as a guide during the conversation.

3. **Talk to them in person or call them:** If you feel ready to confront them about your feelings, you can choose to meet

with them in person or call them to have an open and honest conversation. This approach allows for immediate interaction and can provide an opportunity for them to respond.

4. **Keep or get rid of the letter:** You might decide to keep the raw letter as a reminder of your emotional journey and growth, preserve it in your journal, or hide it away. Alternatively, if you feel that writing the raw letter was enough for your healing process, you can choose to get rid of it, symbolizing the release of those emotions. You can tear it to shreds, burn it, or do anything else that feels right to you.

The one thing I do not recommend you do is simply give them the raw letter. It embodies your rawness, a display of complete transparency and vulnerability. Revealing all of your innermost thoughts and feelings leaves you emotionally exposed, like being utterly naked, with no protection from their potential responses or actions. The raw letter was meant for your eyes only. It serves as a tool for learning how to treat yourself with care when you're vulnerable and in need of healing from past wounds. The raw letter plays a crucial role in helping you deal with and confront your personal issues and emotions head-on. It allows you to finally tell your story by writing it, starting the process of healing. For those reasons, it really isn't a tool for communicating with others, and shouldn't be shared as a result.

But it's also important to properly frame your expectations if you do confront the person the letter was directed to (regardless of the form that confrontation takes). Often, many of us engage in behaviors, actions, and conversations with others in an attempt to wield influence, predict outcomes, or provoke reactions, all while operating under the guise of a cause-and-effect mentality. We convince ourselves that if we do X, then the other person will surely respond with Y. That is, if I can do this, then s/he will do or say that. Regrettably, in the realm of relationships and interpersonal dynamics, this theory tends to fall short. The truth is, that trying to manipulate outcomes or responses in this manner doesn't yield consistent results.

For someone who has written a raw letter, the right moment for confronting another person is when they are capable of expressing themselves without any expectations and can relinquish the urge to control the reactions of the other person or the eventual outcome. At that juncture (and only at that juncture) are they truly prepared to share their thoughts and convey their feelings.

It's crucial to bear in mind that when we address our issues, our objective is to ultimately release and relinquish the emotional burden we've been carrying. I am encouraging us to give back to that particular person who caused the problems and the weight of the burden we have been carrying. It belongs to them instead of us carrying it all the time. We're passing back these concerns to the individuals who initiated them, as they rightfully belong there, not within us. We often burden ourselves with matters that aren't our responsibility to carry. The essence of this process is to articulate our truths, express our sentiments, and assert ourselves to the person at the core of the problem.

A key takeaway I'd like to emphasize is that through this process of expression, the person you've confronted can no longer maintain ignorance or say they didn't know because you've now expressed how their actions have caused harm and impacted your life. We finally shared with them how they hurt us and how that has affected our lives.

But it's essential to understand in that process that once we've spoken our truth, the onus shifts to them on how they choose to respond. I won't sugarcoat or give a false sense of hope for the potential outcomes or offer you unrealistic expectations about how the other person might react. We can't exert control over their handling of our truths. Our primary responsibility lies in communicating our concerns to the person who has hurt us or with whom we have an issue.

It's crucial to remember that while we can't control or manage their reactions, we can certainly regulate and control our own. Before we extend vulnerability to others, we must first make peace with the notion of being vulnerable within ourselves. If you aren't comfortable or at ease with your own internal vulnerability, extending it outward to another individual will undoubtedly prove challenging. The raw letter, however, becomes a tool to aid in cultivating that internal vulnerability. It helps with being vulnerable with yourself first. I urge you to pay close attention and practice mindfulness as you navigate how you treat yourself during these instances of both internal and external vulnerability.

Remember, whatever you decide, it's essential to prioritize your well-being and emotional health. If you feel overwhelmed or find it challenging to cope with your emotions, consider seeking support from a trusted friend, family member, or a professional counselor or therapist who can help guide you through the process.

Chapter 7

A Closer Look at Validation and Processing

A Case Study in Dealing

LET me illustrate the importance of validation and the raw letter process by going deep into them with a real-life example. One of my clients, Angie, had been grappling with deep-rooted issues concerning both of her parents. Her feelings toward her father were filled with strong dislike, while she harbored significant irritation toward her mother. When Angie first sought therapy, she was struggling with a persistent fear of losing her job, a fear exacerbated by a history of being fired from previous positions. As we processed her fears and examined her reality, it became evident her struggles extended beyond her job-related anxieties.

Angie had experienced a profound loss in her life, the absence of a healthy mother-daughter relationship, and also a damaged father-daughter relationship bond. Through our therapeutic conversations, I began to probe and inquire about the reasons for her anger toward her parents, and she revealed and opened up about the hurt and resentment she felt due to their actions in different ways. Angie shared that her mother had been deeply unhappy due to mistreatment from her father, and as a result, her mother became emotionally distant and unavailable to Angie. This lack of physical, emotional, and mental presence from her mother had a deep impact on Angie's life.

At the age of 5, she had a vivid memory that left a lasting impact on her emotional development. She was frightened by a dream related to a distressing incident at school and called out to her mother for comfort and reassurance. However, her mother disregarded her pleas and merely brushed off her concerns, telling her everything would be fine. Angie felt a deep sense of hurt as her mother failed to console her, ask about her dream, or offer protection. She realized that she couldn't depend on her mother for emotional support, and this belief continued to shape her interactions with her parents.

As she grew older, Angie found herself seeking attention, affection, love, and connection from her mother, but she was denied. Her mother would often be preoccupied with her own unhappiness and issues. Angie took the role of her mother's protector, which caused her to develop resentment toward her father. She didn't like how her father treated her mother, neglecting her and not appreciating her. Wanting to make her mother smile and ensure her well-being, Angie stepped up to her father to confront him to defend her. Unfortunately, this responsibility made her increasingly irritated with her mother, wondering why she couldn't stand up for herself. She recognized that she needed her mother, but her mother needed her more.

As Angie reached adulthood, she realized that both parents had significantly negatively affected her life. She didn't like how their dynamic had shaped her and how her mother remained trapped in an unhappy marriage. Despite being there for her, she felt that her mother never reciprocated and instead made everything about herself. Any attempt to talk to her mother about her own issues was met with indifference, leaving Angie feeling unimportant once again.

Her mother still calls Angie to complain about her father, but Angie feels frustrated that she does nothing to change the situation. Moreover, when Angie tries to open up about her own struggles, her mother redirects the focus back to herself, ignoring Angie's needs and leaving her feeling emotionally neglected. Angie has come to realize that she always feels responsible for taking care of her mother, even when she longs for her mother's support and understanding. The accumulated resentment toward both parents has led to a dislike for both of them and a strong desire to break free from their influence on her life.

Validation

As I actively listened, I acknowledged the weight she has been carrying, the emotional burden of unresolved feelings, and the struggle to maintain interactions with her parents while suppressing the hurt and pain caused by them by not addressing, releasing, or expressing herself. I recognized how overwhelming it must have been for her to act as a protector for her mother for such a significant part of her life. I could sense her pain, both in her words and in the echoes of her 5-year-old inner child. I could feel the profound need within herself to be understood and validated. I could sense her yearning to be loved, heard, seen, and protected as well as her strong desire to feel good enough and valued.

As her tears flowed, I instinctively offered empathy and compassion. I gently urged her to release her emotions and let them out, assuring her that her feelings were valid both in the present and the past. At that moment, I truly saw and acknowledged her. I let Angie know SHE mattered. It was clear that she felt important, and I could sense the weight of that realization on her. I expressed gratitude for her trusting in me and for allowing me to share in her vulnerability. In return, she conveyed her appreciation, mentioning how she felt emotionally exhausted and drained yet pleasantly surprised by her ability to open up, allowing her to express herself, especially since she hadn't confided such sentiments to anyone before.

The Raw Letter

After Angie's question, "What comes next?" I introduced the concept of the raw letter to her. I acknowledged the existence of more within her that needed to be shared, emphasizing the importance of finding a safe space for this expression, a space solely dedicated to her. A space where she could reveal her truths, giving voice to every emotion from past and present. A space created to be devoid of dismissals or counterarguments, not being ignored or hearing rebuttals. A space where she could be unfiltered and authentic, free from apologies. A space where fear and overthinking would lose their grip. A space where crying, waves of anger, pauses, feelings of being overwhelmed, and restarts were all acceptable stages of the process of learning to deal with her emotions.

I motivated her to compose this raw letter addressed to either parent. I asked Angie to choose which parent she wanted to begin with, explaining that this letter was exclusively for her and would not be shared with her parents. This was her special chance to prioritize herself, making it solely about her, unburdening and releasing the pain she had carried for so long. It was time for her to tell her story. The time had come for the narrative to be told. I encouraged Angie to delve deep, encouraging her to confront the truths of her five-year-old self, progressing through the years to teenage and young adult stages.

As concerns arose within her, she stated, "It sounds frightening. What if I lose myself and don't come back?" She was worried about a potentially dark or destabilizing place, expressing fears of going astray and "crazy." In response, I validated her apprehensions, acknowledging the daunting nature of the endeavor. I acknowledged her inclination to suppress and stifle feelings that had existed since her 5-year-old self and up until now. However, I elaborated on how suppressing these feelings had cast a shadow over her life, impacting her in multifaceted ways. I posed the question, "How has keeping it all in serving you? How is that working for you?" Her answer was clear: "It hasn't."

Continuing the conversation, I emphasized the power to proceed at her own pace. Angie possessed the autonomy to dictate the tempo of her journey. When it became too overwhelming or too much, I assured her it was perfectly acceptable to take a break or pause to literally put the pen down.

To drive this point home, I shared with Angie the analogy of a kettle. Much like us, a kettle doesn't shatter or break when exposed to high heat; it simply lets off steam to relieve pressure. The water inside might even boil over, creating a whistling sound. When the water is too hot, we release the "stopper" or lower the heat. That's exactly what I was asking Angie to do.

I urged her to release her emotions and thoughts, let them flow, and ease off when they become overwhelming, just as you would take a break from writing. She acknowledged this with a nod, confirming she understood the analogy.

During the session, I expressed my belief that it is apparent that there's a need for her to heal from her past relationship with her parents before she can establish a healthy relationship with them now. I outlined my intentions behind the concept of the raw letter for Angie, hoping that she would permit herself into her feelings. I encouraged her to write about her past desires as well as her current needs from each of her parents. Furthermore, I emphasized that the raw letter could offer her an opportunity to ponder why both parents had difficulties establishing a loving relationship with her. Its purpose was to serve as a channel to articulate the sense of neglect and abandonment she felt from them at various points. Angie thought deeply about what I was proposing and finally said, "I want to give it a shot. I will write it."

The Outcome

You might be anticipating a triumphant conclusion to Angie's story, but it's important to grasp that creating the raw letter isn't a simple task. In fact, it took Angie several months before she even embarked on writing the letter to her mother. Throughout this period, we had weekly sessions where we examined the reasons behind her reluctance. She frequently reported a lack of time or forgetfulness, which were actually indicators of her not feeling, manifesting through avoidance. In response, I demonstrated understanding and patience, validating her feelings while helping her internalize these qualities in herself. I gently reminded her that there was no universally right or wrong timing. When she truly felt prepared, that is when the letter would come to fruition. And indeed, it eventually did.

The catalyst was an incident where her mother became extremely upset with her father, and Angie needed her mother's support. Unfortunately, her mother didn't lend an ear, causing Angie immense frustration. This became the trigger that initiated the writing of the raw letter.

Because Angie had identified and sat with her feelings, she could articulate her thoughts with remarkable eloquence in the raw letter, which she shared during one of our therapy sessions. As she read it aloud, tears streamed down her face. It was as if I could witness the release of steam and pent-up emotions, a validation of her feelings, and the emergence of newfound clarity.

Upon concluding the reading of the letter, she uttered, "Now I see the reason behind your suggestion. I understand the weight I have been carrying for the majority of my life. I'm experiencing a newfound lightness. I'm liberated and unburdened. It is as if I've set my emotions free and allowed myself to be heard – by none other than myself. I hadn't truly comprehended the depth of my hurt or how extensively it impacted my life. I hadn't realized the need for healing."

"While I was writing it, I was engulfed by a wave of emotions. I welled up, cried, yelled, and felt anger, sadness, and even disgust. But there was also an underlying sense of relief. I kept pouring my thoughts onto the paper, occasionally taking breaks that spanned several days. Yet, I always returned to it, understanding that the process wasn't over. I wasn't finished. But being in this moment, reading it aloud today, I'm actually listening to my own words, my emotions, and my thoughts. It is so powerful. It's an incredibly potent and therapeutic experience for me. I hadn't recognized how much I needed this."

Curious about her plans after unearthing her truth through the raw letter, I asked what steps she intended to take, spelling out some of the options. As she embarked on this next phase, she shared, "I'm going to compose a letter, using the raw letter as a reference, to convey my feelings to my mother. However, I won't actually give it to her, as I don't believe she'd handle it well. Yet, I do plan to share some key points with her. I hope that she'll be receptive and gain an understanding of my feelings." Inquiring about her expectations, I highlighted that if she intended to read the letter to her mother expecting to elicit change or a reaction, it might be best to wait. If she planned to read the letter for that reason, it would have been wise to defer addressing these matters with her mother until a later time. It's important to acknowledge that Angie's mother was previously unaware of her daughter's emotions and experiences. Through the sharing of her feelings, this understanding has now surfaced. However, it is vital to remember that Angie doesn't possess the ability to control, dictate, or govern how her mother will respond or act in the aftermath of this revelation.

Since then, Angie began to interact with her mother differently. She accepted the fact that she can't regulate or control how her mother reacts or changes, but Angie can control how she changes and interacts with her mother. Angie revealed that she stopped allowing her mother's behaviors to affect her the same way. Although her mother didn't respond to her expressing herself, she learned a lot about herself. She began to take responsibility for herself. By trusting in the therapeutic process, Angie was engulfed in the healing process.

I encourage each of you to understand how allowing yourself to feel and sit with those emotions is a part of the healing process. You can also learn to validate your emotions by professing that your emotions are valuable and important. You need to validate how your experiences and thoughts matter as you permit yourself to begin to process your feelings, experiences, and thoughts by writing the raw letter.

One of the wonderful aspects of the raw letter is that it provides an opportunity for you to express and feel your emotions while validating yourself. Writing the raw letter may or may not sound daunting to some, but I have seen many individuals embark on the healing journey through these techniques. I employ you to give it a try. Stand in your truth and release it. My primary concern is YOUR well-being and your journey toward HEALING. This process and the choices you make following validation and the raw letter are forms of healing within themselves. Remember, it's a moment where you are finally confronting and dealing with the wound and allowing yourself to be open and vulnerable.

Chapter 8

How Do You DEAL Through Exploring Your Inner Child?

Your Inner Child

ANOTHER intervention and approach for dealing with emotions that I incorporate into certain sessions involves helping my clients discover, explore, identify, and acknowledge their inner child. This concept was initially formed by psychologist Carl Jung (1875-1961), who is often credited with coining the term "inner child." Among the various archetypes defined by Jung, the inner child is one of them. He associated this inner child with memories of innocence, playfulness, creativity, and a sense of optimism for the future. According to Dr. Diana Raab, "Each one of us has an inner child or way of being," and this inner child plays a significant role in the process of individuation.[18] The idea of an inner child, a childlike essence within us, has both psychological origins and a presence in pop culture. Over time, Jungian archetypes have been embraced by the New Age movement.

In simpler terms, I firmly believe that each of us possesses an inner child. This internal essence represents the boy or girl within us, seeking attention, love, assistance, acceptance, celebration, affection, and acknowledgment. It doesn't always stem from experiences of hurt, pain, or fear. I encourage you to embark on a journey of exploration – to acquaint yourself with your inner self. Within each of us resides an inner child who seeks attention and care. During those instances when you experience childlike inclinations, a longing, a potent desire, or an emotional surge, I encourage you to initiate

18 Crystal Raypole, "Finding and Getting to Know Your Inner Child," Healthline.com, accessed February 12, 2020, https://www.healthline.com/health/inner-child.

a self-evaluation or introspection. Ask yourself what might be occurring internally and what you may need. I understand this may be challenging to articulate, let alone identify. Remember, it's these moments when an inner need is calling out. It's those instances when you've tried various external remedies like eating, drinking, smoking, partying, or engaging in sexual activity. Yet, these actions fail to satisfy or fulfill that internal need and longing.

Delving and tapping into your inner child becomes essential when the pursuits of spending money, consuming alcohol, using marijuana, gambling, eating, or busying yourself fail to fill the void. These activities often leave you with a sense of emptiness, a feeling that something is amiss or not quite right. By allowing ourselves to reflect, I believe we can unravel our inner child's presence. At times, this might manifest as emotions like loneliness, fear, invisibility, hurt, disappointment, neglect, ignored, overlooked, or being forgotten. In these instances, we need to turn our focus inward and attend to ourselves, inquire about our current state, and understand our needs.

Another way of thinking about what you are doing is envisioning connecting with your soul. Pose questions to your inner self, such as which childhood aspects or thoughts are prevailing at this moment. What does my inner self truly require right now? What do I really need at this moment? Typically, the yearnings of this inner child align with the age at which the initial hurt occurred or the first vivid memory of immense joy emerged. For instance, it might relate to a time when you were 7, 12, or 17 years old. Paying keen attention to those thoughts, emotions, and sensations that surface and are a burst of lightheartedness or the need for attention. Strive to discern what your inner self needs in that instance: it could be a hug, an engaging activity, recognition, a comedic movie, laughter, tranquility, or fostering a connection with your inner child through journaling.

To help illustrate the concept of the inner child, I encourage each of you to connect with your own inner self and emphasize its positive aspects; let me share and divulge some of my own pleasant experiences with my inner child as I learned to deal with my feelings before we explore the not-so-pleasant ones.

I'm deeply connected with my inner child – my little Marcella – a part of me I've come to know very well. I spend considerable time nurturing and engaging with her. I actively listen to her presence and can discern when she surfaces, especially when I feel a yearning, eagerness, or a craving for childlike activities. It's during these times that I recognize she requires my attention. I have a strong yearning for sorbet, which is when little Marcella radiates joy, jumps with excitement, giggles, and sings. Another moment is when I watch certain types of movies to fellowship with my inner self. I feel an indescribable elation as I connect with the characters on the screen. Often, these movies trigger memories from my childhood. This experience invokes a sense of tranquility and peace, even during moments of emotional complexity or vulnerability.

But there are other times that I delve into my inner self, exploring the full spectrum of emotions she (essentially, me) might be undergoing – particularly the powerful emotion of fear. Fear and other feelings, in their intensity, serve as indicators, prompting me to internally check-in, recognize, and connect with my inner child. For example, when I was at the age of ten, this time encapsulates a period of feeling abandoned, sorrowful, sad, hurt, perplexed, wounded, inadequate, and angry. These emotions surfaced when my father left due to my parents' decision to separate. Despite him maintaining communication and attempting to sustain a relationship with my sister and me, I still perceived their separation as a form of abandonment. The family unit I adored had been dismantled. The pain of their divorce was profound.

These instances that trigger feelings of neglect prompt me to reconnect with my inner child. The emotions of fear, feeling unloved, blaming myself for their divorce, and betrayal surface. During those moments, I reach out to that fragment of myself and reaffirm my affection for the younger Marcella. I take a moment to convey to all aspects of myself that despite the pain or apprehension I was facing, I remained resilient. I assure the 10-year-old Marcella that history won't repeat itself. I reminded her that WE are safe, dispelling any echoes of the past. I remind "little Marcella" that she is not her mother or her father. They are humans who made mistakes. Yet, within their choices, they loved her. My father tirelessly attempted to sustain and maintain a connection and a relationship with me. Regrettably, my younger self chose to rebel and push him away, shunning him during mandatory visits. Anger toward my father especially surged since I lived with my mother and not him. It was extraordinarily hard for me to comprehend the impact on me at 16 when he passed away. Understanding was beyond my grasp.

The pain caused by his passing surpassed even the ache stemming from their decision to separate. His death coincided with a time when I harbored resentment toward him, making his departure even more poignant. The chance to express thoughts and emotions I yearned to convey while he was alive and tried to communicate with me now eluded me. I held back from disclosing the depth of my pain. I was puzzled and hurt, knowing that he would never hear my words and I would never hear his voice again. My pain and loss ran deep. Still, my affection and love for him endured, regardless of it all.

The Importance of Connecting With Your Inner Child

As we connect with our inner child or self, we achieve a greater sense of wholeness within. We initiate a journey of self-discovery, embracing the various facets of ourselves that we often overlook or deny. This process of acquainting ourselves with our diverse aspects and truths leads us toward a more fulfilled state, gradually dispelling the sense of void and emptiness. A sense of completeness takes root within us as we learn to attune ourselves to that inner voice that explains our sadness or unravels the reasons behind our strong reactions to a friend's words. These instances often trigger our inner child, longing for the love and care it may not have received during its developmental years or seeking specific comfort required in that very moment. Some instances may come when we want to experience happiness to avoid feeling empty and unhappy. If we think about our childhood, most of us yearned to be loved and to feel happy. "I want to be happy" is a common statement often expressed and heard. We often search for happiness in many ways.

Many clients share that they experience happiness while traveling, shopping, spending time with their significant others, or engaging in exercise. However, what these examples all have in common is that one's happiness tends to be contingent on external circumstances. Often, we consciously choose to evoke feelings of happiness by entertaining humorous, light-hearted, or positive thoughts. Engaging in enjoyable activities, socializing with friends and family, pursuing our favorite hobbies, and even indulging in certain habits like smoking, drinking, gambling, sex, eating, shopping, stealing, and taking pills can trigger moments of happiness. All these instances explain how happiness is closely tied to specific circumstances, illustrating its situational nature. As I often say, in these instances, "Happiness is based on what is happening." Unfortunately, it doesn't heal us from our deep wounds. Focusing on our happiness can be a distraction from dealing with the root of issues and posing as a temporary solution.

I believe that there is an inherent desire for profound connections that resides within us that is more important than our search for happiness. As humans, we yearn for deep connections, not just fleeting happiness. We have the potential to delve into avenues that lead us to experience states of joy, inner peace, and contentment. These states reflect transient happiness and the state of our overall being, which I believe is essential in this healing journey.

One way to access joy, inner peace, and contentment is by establishing harmony with our inner child, exploring and engaging in introspection to unravel our inner selves. By going deeper into profound questions, we gain insights into our nature in a manifestation of self-love.

In moments of solitude, when the pangs of loneliness arise, I encourage you to investigate the yearnings that lie beneath. It becomes paramount to identify these desires and discern the underlying issues that contribute to feelings of isolation. Having identified these issues, I advocate for meeting these unmet needs. The process involves learning how to fulfill the longings that resonate within us, which is an excellent example of self-love.

How Self-Love Manifests

Embracing self-love is an extraordinary means of connecting with our inner child. To love oneself equates to cultivating an affectionate bond and love with that inner child or inner self. This journey entails embarking upon a path of accepting every facet of our existence. Often, individuals identify themselves through specific labels such as "type A personality," "problem solver," "sensitive," "caring," "procrastinator," or "enforcer." These labels showcase how we tend to emphasize certain aspects of ourselves while remaining less aware of other dimensions.

In my conversations with clients, I stress that we extend beyond the labels and roles we assume. Our makeup encompasses a spectrum of qualities with multiple extremes ranging from caring, loving, and sharing to procrastinating, fearing, controlling, being type A personality, exhibiting elements of narcissism, understanding, vindictiveness, obsessiveness, possessiveness, loyalty, being a great friend, being unavailable, and exhibiting guardedness.

Often, we use compartmentalization as a means of self-preservation, a defense mechanism aimed at safeguarding our emotional well-being and protection. Compartmentalization involves segmenting ourselves, others, or situations into distinct sections or categories. While this approach helps us to focus on specific aspects, many of us could benefit from a holistic understanding of our various behaviors, personalities, and traits. It is crucial for us to perceive ourselves as complete entities, a composite of diverse parts. I refer to this concept as your "total self."

I encourage each of you to take an introspective journey, looking at the comprehensive parts of your existence. This involves acknowledging all the diverse facets that constitute your identity. By recognizing that we are more than singular parts, personalities, or behaviors, we can begin to see ourselves in our totality. My encouragement is for everyone reading this book to embark on this internal exploration, cultivating an equitable understanding of every facet of "self" and, therefore, evolving into a holistic and complete version of oneself.

How can I cultivate affection for every aspect of myself? How can I embrace my "total self" with all its components? How do I learn how to love all of my many parts as a whole? Connecting with your inner child can answer these questions and it is a demonstration of self-love that is intricately woven into the process of healing. Doing so ultimately guides us to the third and final step – **HEAL**ing.

Chapter 9

Healing One Hurt at a Time

What it Means to Heal

THE final stage is to heal, which is the last step of the overall transformative process discussed throughout this book. We learned how to FEEL by identifying our emotions and truly asking ourselves how do I REALLY feel.

We learned how to DEAL and confront our thoughts and emotions by giving them space, sitting with them and validating them as well as working through the underlying event. By first acknowledging our emotions and then addressing them paves the way for healing. "We feel, then deal, in order to heal."

Healing isn't a straightforward journey. The path to healing may be arduous, yet it's a necessary and pivotal undertaking. Although healing might prompt discomfort and apprehension, its benefits are undeniably rewarding and profound.

We are tender. Consider envisioning and imagining a scenario where we care for our hearts, minds, and souls in the same manner we attend to the physical scars and wounds we've successfully healed from. This perspective leads me to believe that our world could be a significantly better place with a focus on emotional healing. Moreover, I am confident that you, the individual reading this book, would experience considerable personal growth.

It's common for individuals to claim they don't know how to embark on the healing process or tend to their wounds. Yet this notion is misleading and a false truth. Many of us are well-versed in caring for our dear ones. Throughout our lives, we've cared for people in numerous ways, playing an integral role in their healing journeys. This very fact stands as evidence that we possess the capability to nurture and mend our own wounds. So, even if you feel uncertain about it, I urge you to recognize that you do, in fact, hold this ability.

Like you, I too had to learn to extend the same principles I apply to others toward my own healing journey. While fear lingers, I recognize my capability to undertake this endeavor, considering my history of assisting numerous individuals. Just as those individuals sought my support, I find myself in need of my own care even more. No exemption applies here. I rightfully deserve the identical devotion, concentration, and allegiance I've dedicated to others.

The explanation you've observed illustrates how thoughts can be transformed into alternative statements, capturing one's truth with a positive perspective. These alternative viewpoints promote equilibrium and balance and help bridge the gap between extremes. There is power in our words and thoughts. The strength of words and thoughts is undeniable. By reshaping our thinking, we possess the potential to genuinely alter our behaviors and emotions. Transforming the path we are on allows us to think differently and can lead to changes in our behaviors and feelings. Our healing experiences are molded by our beliefs. Because our thoughts have power, we possess the capacity to guide our cognitive processes and perceptions on a journey of healing.

Reviewing the Steps

In the preceding chapters, we've outlined two critical steps that pave the way for healing. This chapter serves as a practical guide, urging each of you to actively engage with the steps outlined in the earlier chapters. This is where I encourage every reader to experiment with these strategies, transforming theory into action.

Consider whether you have been able to pinpoint the sources of your hurts, wounds, pain, disappointments, struggles, experiences of loss, or any lingering challenges that need healing. Identify the areas in need of healing. I understand that this might pose a challenge, but it's essential to give them due recognition rather than dismissing them. Take a pause and utilize this moment to jot down or type your initial reflections about the primary wound that surfaces.

____

____

____

____

____

____

____

____

____

____

____

____

____

Now, describe your emotions. Share what you are feeling about that particular wound.

____

____

____

____

____

Now, let's truly immerse ourselves in those emotions. Take the time to delve into why that specific emotion has taken root within you and explore the underlying reasons. As you delve deeper into your inner self, seek to identify the core issue that's exerting its influence. This could pertain to what transpired, what didn't happen, the missed opportunities, losses incurred, or unfulfilled desires. Take this moment to answer these questions earnestly, enhancing your connection with your feelings and the wounds they've unearthed. This step involves allowing yourself to sit with your emotions and the wounds, which paves the way for the subsequent step of addressing them. Remember, this phase entails acknowledging your feelings and experiences without judgment.

Let's proceed to validate your feelings and experiences. It's time to process the events that unfolded. What aspects are you holding onto? What lies at the core of the pain you're grappling with? That lingering feeling you've been attempting to suppress and ignore. It's time to address it. Now, consider your thoughts on forgiving both yourself and the individuals responsible for perpetuating the pain you are currently feeling. I recognize that this might evoke discomfort, yet you are courageous for facing these emotions.

As we navigate this journey, I encourage you all to process your emotions, the experiences you encountered, and your contemplations by expressing them through writing. This process doesn't have to conform strictly to the traditional notion of journaling; it's more about embracing a medium that facilitates transparency and the release of pent-up emotions.

Let's take it a little further, which brings me to the following point. Before addressing our wounds with others, we must address them within ourselves. How did we go about this internal confrontation? How did we tend to the wound? How did we administer care? How did we evaluate both ourselves and the pain itself? Did we inadvertently shove it back into our own faces? It's crucial to assess your responses to these inquiries to gauge if you've genuinely confronted these wounds within yourself.

To begin, it's important to recognize and understand that these suggestions are part of a larger process. Just as none of us transformed into who we are overnight, healing won't occur overnight either. The accumulation of years' worth of hurts, letdowns, wounds, and traumas has shaped each of us. As a result, the time frame for healing can vary widely depending on the nature of the wounds.

Furthermore, it's essential to acknowledge the sources of our pain, who inflicted it, who hurt us, the reasons for its impact, and the current pain. This calls for an honest look in the mirror.

It is vital to recognize that we can't tend to all our wounds simultaneously. We must consciously choose which pain to address, allowing the healing process to unfold. To navigate this, we need to approach each wound methodically, tackling them one by one.

One of my clients, Verse, recognized and identified a total of 36 emotional hurts as well as wounds that she had been carrying and desperately needed to address. As the weight of these hurts became overwhelming, Verse attempted to tackle all these wounds simultaneously, a pursuit that proved to be unattainable. Recognizing how hard this approach was, I encouraged her to approach her emotional pain differently by compartmentalizing each hurt. In essence, I proposed breaking down her emotional wounds into distinct sections or categories.

Consequently, she decided to start her healing journey by addressing the loss of her father a decade ago and examining their relationship leading up to his passing. This shift towards focusing on one specific emotional wound at a time yielded positive outcomes. She conveyed her experience of how impactful this intervention was for her, highlighting the immense benefits she gained from this approach.

Friendly Reminder Why Healing Matters

Remember, the aftermath of not undergoing healing can manifest in various ways. We might engage in self-sabotage, become trapped in a sense of stagnation or feeling stuck, and resort to self-medication through substances like drugs, alcohol, sex, gambling, or emotional eating. Similarly, busying ourselves excessively, harboring jealousy, making unfavorable comparisons, and finding a shared space where misery loves company all constitute potential outcomes.

This notion aligns with the well-known mantra that carries timeless truth: "Hurt people hurt people, and wounded individuals inadvertently inflict wounds upon others." A cascade of consequences can unfurl, such as inner devastation, self-hatred, self-loathing, simmering anger, eroded trust, a defensive and guarded demeanor, a life devoid of fulfillment, confusion, a lack of direction, bewildering uncertainty, and an overall sense of stagnation.

Furthermore, this trajectory could lead to disillusionment, profound distress, an internal void, an overwhelming feeling of emptiness, a pervasive sense of being misunderstood and mistreated, the adoption of a victim mentality, assuming the role of the antagonist or a villain, nurturing bitterness, fostering resentment, and becoming emotionally detached.

My client Barbara was headed down this dangerous path until she decided it was time to heal. During our sessions, Barbara identified several individuals such as her mother, father, a teacher from the past, and her current husband who had inflicted hurt upon her. I guided her toward verbalizing the specific ways in which each of these individuals had caused her pain. As tears traced paths down her cheeks, dampening her pristine white shirt, she began to share her sentiments. "My mother hurt me," she recounted, her voice trembling, "by remaining emotionally distant and engrossed in her work. She was absent during pivotal moments when I needed her guidance for friendships, relationships, and conflicts with teachers. I perpetually felt unseen and unheard, especially when I craved her words of affirmation, my worthiness." Barbara's need for validation was profound.

She shared how her father's infidelity shattered her sense of security, leading him to abandon their family for another woman. "I felt abandoned and deserted by him," she confessed, her vulnerability evident. "I internalized a belief of not being good enough for him to stay, a sensation of being unloved and unimportant. I unfairly bore the weight of blame, repeatedly questioning what I did wrong. I remember pleading and sobbing, imploring him not to leave me, but my cries were met with silence." Amid the distress she felt, Barbara recalled a teacher who had dismissed her potential, deeming her insignificant due to missed assignments. The teacher's callousness coincided with a period of distraction in school which was precipitated by her father's departure and amplified her feelings of invisibility and despair.

Lastly, Barbara shared the most recent source of her pain: her husband, who had been engaged in infidelity for years. "My deepest fear happened in my marriage," she admitted with a heavy sigh, capturing the deep anguish that had been compounded over time.

As I acknowledged and validated Barbara's hurt and pain, I ensured that she felt truly seen, heard, and secure during the session. Her tears began to flow, and her vulnerability became obvious. At that moment, she revealed that she carried a multitude of wounds within her. This realization was a shared human experience. We all bear our own wounds that require healing.

Guiding her gently, I encouraged Barbara to select a single hurt to focus on, emphasizing the importance of addressing wounds one by one. This approach prevents the overwhelming feeling that can arise from tackling multiple issues simultaneously. Research supports the notion that focusing on a single task at a time enhances productivity. Hence, I reiterated the significance of addressing one wound at a time for effective healing.

Although Barbara exhibited initial reluctance, she eventually chose to begin with the wound inflicted by her teacher. I urged her to start by acknowledging the wound to herself, recognizing its overall impact. Subsequently, I advised her to journal about the incident, delving into the ways her teacher's words and actions had caused harm. Through this process, Barbara confronted the array of emotions tied to her teacher's hurtful behavior, sensations of embarrassment, disrespect, insignificance, hurt, and scolding. This first step marked the beginning of her healing journey.

As she sat with these emotions, Barbara explored further into the healing process. This involved addressing the situation, her own feelings, the teacher's role, and the triggers it unearthed within her. In subsequent sessions, I encouraged Barbara to compose a raw letter addressed to her teacher, marking another step in her healing process.

At our next session, Barbara brought the raw letter with her. As she read it aloud, tears flowed freely. It was as if she had finally connected with her inner child, particularly the version of herself at age 12. Through the letter, she granted her inner child a voice that she actively listened to and cared for. Barbara decided to send her teacher an email detailing the impact of her words and actions, urging her to recognize the profound influence she has as an educator. Barbara's email also highlighted the negative effects she had endured even after 25 years.

Reflecting on her journey, Barbara shared, "I feel a sense of relief, liberation, empowerment, and lightness." This experience of completing a therapeutic task and/or goal highlighted the importance of recognizing our emotions and celebrating our accomplishments, victories, and proud moments, offering ourselves genuine congratulations and a figurative pat on the back.

Celebrate and Pat Your Back

Hearing Barbara's story, hopefully, brings a smile to your face – a testament to the victories you should be celebrating like Barbara. I emphasize behaviors like self-pride by teaching clients to revel in their accomplishments during our sessions.

One approach I've named is "pat yourself on your back," a celebratory and self-appreciation gesture. It involves acknowledging one's progress and growth, stepping out of one's comfort zone, being uncomfortable, or any other moments of pride. In these instances, I encourage my clients to highlight what they've achieved, expressed, or undertaken. I then prompt them to physically pat their own backs during our session. This simple action often elicits laughter initially, but after a moment of hesitation, most clients join in, and their smiles grow into something infectious. As support, I do it with them.

The act of patting one's back is a form of behavioral modification, a rewarding system that reinforces desirable behaviors. It serves as a positive stimulus, sending signals to our brains and creating a pleasurable sensation that we desire to perpetuate. When we learn how to acknowledge and celebrate our victories, big or small, we engage in positive reinforcement. Consequently, we tend to repeat those behaviors that bring about such positive feelings.

I've witnessed clients break into broad smiles and laughter as they pat their backs and acknowledge their achievements by saying, "Good job." I recall an interaction with a client named Tinkia. I congratulated her on a goal she had reached, urging her to genuinely appreciate herself. I instructed her to give herself a literal pat on the back while saying, "Good job." She grinned, chuckled, and followed through. "Good job, Tinkia," she exclaimed while patting herself. I pointed out her radiant smile and inquired about her feelings. She expressed surprise at the positive sensation, a sense of accomplishment, and an improved mood.

Before she moved on to her next task, I advised Tinkia to take a moment to savor her accomplishment. This pause, a brief interlude before jumping to the next item on the list, is vital. Often, we're too hasty, treating our to-dos as check boxes and neglecting the opportunity to be present in the current moment. Taking the time to immerse ourselves in what we've achieved enhances our confidence and self-trust, preparing us for the "next" task with a more solid foundation.

In essence, the act of self-celebration and self-pride is deeply satisfying. The principles of behavioral modification encourage us to utilize rewards to foster positive changes and outcomes, especially within ourselves.

It's now your opportunity to engage in the celebratory technique: give yourself a pat on the back. Take a moment to jot down at least one activity, suggestion, thought, or feeling you've accomplished or experienced from your engagement with this book up to this point.

____

____

____

____

Let's proceed by placing your hand on your back and giving yourself a hearty pat while vocalizing "Good job,___________________ (your name). Good job."

How do you feel at this moment? Hold onto that sensation and make sure to carry it forward as you celebrate further by embracing more desired and suitable behaviors.

Chapter 10

Why Trusting Ourselves and Forgiveness Matters

We Are Not Machines

OUR perception of ourselves is marred by a misguided belief that we function similarly to machines. This conviction extends to our assessment of our capacity and capabilities as being uniform. We believe that our capacity and capability are the same. We erroneously convince ourselves that emotions should not factor in, that we lack the time to deal with and address them, and inadvertently treat ourselves as if we were not human.

The emotional responses sought in these pages cannot materialize unless we actively remind ourselves of our humanity and our need for healing. It is crucial to acknowledge our inherent worthiness as individuals deserving of wholeness and completion. I firmly believe that through the process of healing, we emerge as well-rounded individuals. Healing guides us to accept our imperfections and vulnerabilities as shared aspects of being human.

In this journey towards wholeness, we must grant ourselves the same grace, love, empathy, and gentleness that we readily offer others. While we are often quick to extend empathy and love to others around us, we paradoxically exempt ourselves from such considerations. We exhibit a propensity to provide care and love to others while denying ourselves the same mercy and compassion. This incongruity persists despite possessing our own reservoir of advice and guidance. We fail to take heed of our own advice.

For some, self-criticism runs deep, overshadowing the kindness we extend to others. We assume the role of our harshest critic, a sentiment echoed in the saying, *"We are our worst enemy."* This tendency obstructs our path and impedes our healing journey for an array of reasons. We frequently become the source of our own downfall, often sabotaging our progress unwittingly and subconsciously.

I urge you to step aside from your usual routine and create room for the other aspect of yourself: the part that craves wanting to be heard through expression, the facet that yearns to be acknowledged and seen, the segment of you that aspires to be chosen. Seize the opportunity to apply these methods and techniques that will enable you to embrace the newer version of yourself and authentically delve into the exploration and genuine understanding of your feelings.

Bear in mind that we consist of a myriad of dimensions and many parts. Our intricacies and complexities are inherent, and it is our birthright – our inherent entitlement – to comprehend, learn, cherish, and love them. Embracing this holistic perspective is crucial; it's embracing our entirety. We must learn to accept our total selves.

Failure to do so might lead to the emergence of doubts in others, which, in turn, results in a broader lack of trust. When our ability to trust becomes impaired, we often lead a life characterized by caution and being guarded, striving to safeguard our emotional core and hearts. For example, a woman might exhibit traits like fierceness, "feisty," anger, aloofness, bitterness, or even resentment. Similarly, a man might project insensitivity, unavailability, promiscuity, or self-centeredness. These are all defense mechanisms we deploy to protect ourselves from potential pain, exploitation, mistreatment, disillusionment, and disappointment.

Moreover, in these circumstances, trusting ourselves becomes a challenge due to past errors, erroneous decisions, and permitting undesired actions and influences. The truth is that many individuals grappling with trust issues are actually struggling with a lack of self-trust. In simpler terms, we are apprehensive about relying on ourselves. We don't trust ourselves.

The Importance of Self-Trust

Distrust in ourselves often arises from instances where we've allowed others to inflict pain upon us. We might have stayed in relationships beyond their expiration or have chosen to be with individuals despite knowing better. Opportunities to prevent certain outcomes were within our grasp, yet we failed to seize control. Nurturing self-love is unfamiliar territory, contributing to our muddled judgment that results in a series of errors. Sometimes, it's an unpopular, significant mistake that continues to evade self-forgiveness. We tend not to know how to love ourselves by not trusting ourselves.

Our path occasionally steers toward turmoil as we opt for actions that prove detrimental to our well-being. Some find themselves trapped in relationships due to apprehensions about the unknown, an unwillingness to relinquish the positive aspects as well as the good parts, and the daunting prospect of starting anew. The fear of placing trust in another individual looms greatly, given the substantial danger of enduring fresh wounds.

These instances and examples vividly highlight the significance of understanding our missteps and mistakes, acknowledging the points where we went astray, pinpointing where we deviated from the right path, and comprehending the motives that guided our choices as well as the reasons behind our actions. Through this process and insights, we pave the way and lay the foundation for the transformative act of self-forgiveness, an essential step that cultivates and facilitates the restoration of self-trust. This newfound trust in ourselves becomes the stepping stone upon which we can learn to trust others authentically and profoundly. The journey of trusting others commences with the foundation of self-trust. We can begin to trust others when we start trusting ourselves.

In the quest to nurture and build self-trust, bolstering and enhancing our self-confidence and cultivating a robust sense of self-assurance is essential. This implies embracing a mindset where decisions are made thoughtfully, after careful consideration, and aligned with our most discerning judgment. Making well-informed, thoughtful decisions based on our best judgment fosters confidence in our choices. By consistently acting in ways grounded in our values and knowledge, we reinforce the foundation of self-assuredness.

Equally important is the power of association. Our trust can flourish by surrounding ourselves with individuals who authentically live fulfilling and purposeful lives and align with their true selves. When we witness these like-minded individuals pursuing goals that mirror our aspirations, their determination and drive ignite a spark within us, motivating and inspiring us to continually manifest our best selves as we navigate and persevere the intricate tapestry of life. In other words, we can encourage ourselves to continue to show up as our best selves as we live this thing—we all call life.

Trust cascades its influence across multiple facets of our existence. It serves as a cornerstone not only for our relationship with ourselves but also for fostering meaningful connections with family, loved ones, friends, coworkers, colleagues, and humanity at large.

The Power of Forgiveness

I consider it of utmost importance to emphasize and incorporate the concept of forgiveness. Forgiveness stands as an integral element within the healing process. It becomes imperative not only to pardon those who have wronged, harmed, or let us down but also to extend forgiveness to ourselves for permitting individuals or situations to inflict pain upon us.

This acknowledgment extends to comprehending the anguish we inflict upon ourselves through our own actions, leading to self-disappointment. The wrath we often direct toward others can frequently be an expression of our own anger at ourselves. It's not uncommon for our frustration to be directed inward toward what we did or didn't do, what we allowed, chose to abstain from, uttered, refrained from saying, ignored, or disregarded. These instances are indicative of areas where we might require self-forgiveness.

As I advocate for introspection regarding our trust-related struggles and challenges and their origins, I urge you to set aside time to grant both yourself and others forgiveness. This liberating act grants you the autonomy, capacity, and potential to bestow forgiveness and thus embark on a path of deliverance and freedom.

Forgiveness releases us from the chains of resentment and hurt. It serves as a bridge, connecting us to the freeing realms of understanding and empathy. Just as self-trust is a cornerstone, so is forgiveness, for it grants us the power to heal wounds, transcend limitations, and forge connections that are genuine and profound. In extending forgiveness to ourselves, we create a fertile ground for self-trust to flourish anew. By embracing forgiveness for others, we unburden ourselves from the weight of past transgressions, paving the way for a future rich with harmonious relationships and inner peace.

The journey of trust and forgiveness intertwines in a dance of liberation and growth. As you reflect on your own experiences and challenges with trust, remember the transformative potential of self-forgiveness and the expansive power of granting forgiveness to others. Through this process, you unlock the boundless capacity to trust, trust yourself, trust others, and trust in the beautiful medley of human connections.

Spirituality and Healing

One way to make ongoing progress in self-trust and forgiveness is to turn to spirituality. The belief in a higher power – a being attuned to our need for trust and compassion – also aids in the process of healing. When we find it difficult to see beyond our limitations, I've come to realize that having faith in something greater than ourselves is key. This faith in your higher power or the universe can be a source of strength even during the most challenging, unthinkable, and unbearable times. As the saying goes, *"He will make a way out of no way."* Having the conviction, belief, and faith that things will work out or that you'll find strength through your higher power can be incredibly reassuring. Knowing that there's a force more significant and more potent than you that can assist you in any circumstance is comforting.

Research shows that fostering a spiritual connection plays a vital role in the healing journey. According to a study by the National Institutes of Health, religion and spirituality can be advantageous when coping with the aftermath of trauma. According to the study, "Positive religious coping equips individuals to navigate situations where they confront the limits of human power and control and face their own vulnerability and finiteness."[19]

I've observed that spirituality has been a significant source of support for individuals who were receptive to processing their emotions and experiences, ultimately aiding in their healing. For example, one of my clients, Ron, faced numerous losses, disappointments, and hardships. Losing his mother at the tender age of 12, he lacked the nurturing and affectionate presence that a mother provides. This early loss led to feelings of abandonment, deep pain, emptiness, and a sense of brokenness. He tried to compensate by seeking external validation through relationships with women, attempting to fill the void of his mother's absence. He was subconsciously trying to create a new attachment to receive the maternal love and connection he longed for.

Unfortunately, this approach only led to more heartache as he continuously pursued love and affirmation externally. One significant blow was his first love, his high school sweetheart, who left him. This heartbreak triggered a pattern of people-pleasing behavior, where he sought validation by putting others' needs before his own.

---

[19] Rezvan Ameli, Ninet Sinaii, María José Luna, Julia Cheringal, Brunilde Gril, and Ann Berger, "The National Institutes of Health Measure of Healing Experience of All Life Stressors (NIH-HEALS): Factor Analysis and Validation," Plos One 13, no. 12, (December 2018), https://doi.org/10.1371/journal.pone.0207820.

He believed by being needed, he could prevent people from leaving him. Sadly, his belief and the manner in which he related to others led him to experience more hurt and disappointments, leading him to think that people were merely using him, leaving him feeling abused, unseen, lonely, and not good enough.

Despite achieving multiple successes, including a high-paying job, marriage, children, and material possessions such as an expensive home and luxury cars, Ron still grappled with an unshakable sense of emptiness. He still wasn't able to fulfill the void. Throughout his life, he constantly felt like he was chasing the next big thing, leaving him constantly feeling unfulfilled and lacking purpose. Nothing made that feeling of "something is missing" disappear.

This feeling persisted until he experienced a turning point when his second marriage fell apart due to infidelity. He began to drink heavily, self-medicating to numb the pain. Unfortunately, these endeavors made his life worse.

But during his most challenging moment and darkest period, he felt the Holy Spirit reminding him that he was not alone. This moment of despair led him to seek solace in his spirituality. He felt God's presence, warming his "cold and bitter" heart. He was reminded that God can and will fill his feelings of emptiness. He turned to reading the Bible, attending church, meeting with his pastor, seeking therapy, and joining a spiritual support group for men.

Ron's progress has been remarkable. His faith in a higher power sustained him through difficult times, providing the strength he thought he lacked. He's now focused on his internal and spiritual growth as part of his healing journey. He has emphasized to me on multiple occasions that his resilience is directly derived from his faith in God. He acknowledged how blessed and fortunate he was and recognized that God carried and supported him through numerous trying times, particularly when he felt like giving up. During periods of hopelessness, helplessness, despair, and powerlessness, his spirituality became his coping mechanism, his source of hope, his guiding light, and his capacity to overcome all obstacles.

I can relate to this personally as well. My spirituality has prevented me from engaging in maladaptive behaviors, enabling me to overcome challenges and toxic relationships without resorting to negative coping mechanisms such as self-medication.

My hope is for all of us to grasp the dynamics and importance of healing by remembering our shared humanity in this process. Because we are people with inherent dignity, each one of us can address our life experiences, traumas, emotions, and thoughts – to acknowledge and deal with our feelings and allow ourselves an opportunity to heal.

Conclusion

The Role of Therapy

A movie I recently watched involved the true story of a woman's unwavering battle for her children. This divorced woman took a courageous step, leaving behind an abusive husband to shield both herself and her two daughters. Despite their shared custody arrangement, it became evident that he wasn't providing proper care during their time with him. Faced with this grim reality, she confronted him, only to witness him kidnap their young girls.

Despite her attempts to seek legal assistance through the police and her attorney, she encountered frustration and discouragement. It was then she made the pivotal decision to hire a private investigator. This investigator's tenacity led to the discovery of her daughters in Greece, subjected to the torment of physical abuse and neglect at the hands of their father. Driven by unyielding determination, she embarked on a harrowing journey to Greece, determined to rescue and save her children and bring them back to the United States.

Her fierce determination paid off and her triumph was one she rightfully savored. She emerged victorious, securing full custody of her daughters through the legal process. Amid the celebration of her victory, she found a moment of quiet reflection. As she watched her daughters joyfully playing at the park, memories of the arduous journey flooded her mind. Watching them swing on the swings, she couldn't help but express a profound sentiment: "I am so glad they are in therapy." Her words echoed the depth of her motherly concern, acknowledging the healing that her children needed after enduring such traumatic experiences.

Within the pages of this book, I've meticulously outlined and delineated the sequential actions and strategies for the process of healing. I express the importance of how to start the healing journey. I have highlighted the significance of initiating the journey toward healing. Throughout the text, I've used personal anecdotes, clinical insights, data, and resources that have illuminated the efficacy of these steps and explained the beginning of my book's concepts.

However, a prevailing constant factor throughout this book is the role of THERAPY. While embarking on the journey of healing is feasible, it would be an oversight not to highlight the pivotal role that therapy plays in the process. Each of my clients has embarked on their healing journey in our therapeutic relationship. I, too, have navigated the path of healing aided by therapy.

Therapy plays a pivotal role in the journey of healing. Through therapy, our souls find solace and guidance. It teaches us not only to love but also how to love ourselves and receive love. Therapy illuminates our true selves and helps us to see ourselves. It helps us to fulfill the needs we often expect others to meet. Therapy grants us invaluable permission to express our truths and encourages authenticity within us to flourish.

Most of all, therapy offers a platform where individuals can engage in conversations with their therapists, initiating the commencement of their healing journey. It plays an integral and central role in our collective journey to healing. I encourage you to embrace the prospect of embarking on your personal healing process and eventually enlisting the aid of a therapist.

Acknowledging the hurts that have been revealed and identified throughout this book is the first step. We all yearn and need a safe haven where we can express our innermost thoughts and feelings, giving these sentiments a voice-a sanctuary where empathy, compassion, and therapeutic coping skills, mechanisms, and resources coincide.

As we grapple with our emotions – which at times can be overwhelming – professional support becomes imperative to guide our healing voyage. We all need help when we begin to feel, deal, and heal. It's perfectly acceptable to initiate therapy after absorbing the contents of this book. In fact, I would assert that doing so marks the next phase of your action plan after implementing the initial three healing steps and suggested interventions.

Getting Help

The next step in your healing journey is to find and identify a therapist with whom you can cultivate trust, establish a strong rapport, and feel comfortable being open and vulnerable. To begin this process, you can contact your medical insurance provider by calling the 1-800 number listed on the back of your insurance card. Request a list of mental health providers who are in-network.

Alternatively, if you're employed, many companies offer an Employee Assistance Program (EAP), a complimentary service providing their employees access to mental health, substance abuse, legal assistance, and financial literacy resources. This service is often also accessible via a 1-800 number. Contact your Human Resources Department (HR) for the EAP contact number. Usually, most companies collaborate with third-party entities to deliver EAP services, including external and internal counseling and legal aid. It's important to note that any assistance sought, whether internally or externally, remains confidential and cannot be used against you.

Additional resources include crisis intervention hotlines and government helplines. In times of crisis or when you need someone to talk to, you can contact the following numbers for assistance: 1 (866) 359-7953, 1 (800) 273-TALK, and 988.

Some organizations that provide support and services are listed below:

- National Alliance Mental Illness (NAMI) offers crisis counseling, advocacy, resources, and support groups for individuals and families dealing with clinical and chronic mental health challenges. Visit their website, www.nami.org for more information. You can also contact NAMI Chicago Helpline (833) 626-4244 or Text NAMI (6264) to 741741 for 24/7 FREE crisis counseling.

- Mental Health America furnishes educational resources and outreach services to individuals and their families dealing with clinical and chronic mental health issues and diagnoses. Visit their website, www.mhanational.org, for more information.

- Psychology Today provides comprehensive information to help you search for, access, and learn about mental health professionals such as therapists, social workers, and psychologists who use the platform. You can access more detailed information at www.psychologytoday.com.

- The National Institute of Mental Health (NIMH) is a federal agency for research for mental disorders. It conducts and supports research that provides information about mental disorders, a range of related topics, and literature. Visit their website, www.nimh. nih.gov, for more information.

- Grief.com: Because Love Never Dies is a resource for individuals who are dealing with grief and loss through death. It provides support and offers access to grief counseling services.

- Depression and Bipolar Support Alliance provides free support groups, resources, and wellness tools for individuals living with depression or bipolar disorder. Visit their website, www. dbsalliance.org, for more information.

There are internet-based apps available on most computers and smartphones. Additionally, there are local agencies in your area that offer therapy and support.

I make an effort to refer and connect each individual to someone who can help, especially when I'm unable to assist. My intention and aspiration in offering these resources are to alleviate uncertainties like where to seek help or how to find a therapist.

Final Thoughts

You deserve to become the best version of yourself. Becoming a better you translates into being a better partner, parent, sibling, child, friend, lover, colleague, and employer, and fulfilling all the other roles and responsibilities you hold. It is a remarkable journey within the realm of healing.

However, the destination of your journey lies in your hands. It's up to you. Will it continue onward or remain stagnant? My fervent wish for each of you is freedom. Freedom from your past, from your own self-doubt and self-criticism, from those who inflicted harm upon you, from fear, from restrictions and constraints that hold you back, from self-hatred, from self-sabotage, and from the trauma that may have haunted you.

That's my hope and desire for each of you, but it must begin with your own desire. You have to want it for yourself. Make yourself proud, and keep pursuing your healing. You have the capacity to do it. You can do it. You are more than enough. You can change, and the present moment is the perfect time. You can acknowledge your feelings and deal with them in order to heal. It's never too late.

Acknowledgments

I express my sincerest appreciation to my clients, who have consistently and unwaveringly urged me to embark on this writing journey, particularly for this book. Your encouragement to document the therapeutic steps I've suggested and share them with a wider audience has been instrumental. Thank you to those who said, "Marcella, you should write a book. Marcella, that was impactful. I need to feel, to deal in order to heal."

I am especially thankful to those who allowed me to share their experiences and contribute to the insights and lessons shared within these pages. Being part of your journey has been an incredible honor, and I am grateful for the trust you placed in me. Thank you for embracing those emotions we often try to ignore as we navigate the complexities of life. As we all say, this "thing" we call life. Man, these Life Experiences."

I often find myself reflecting on my immense gratitude for each of you who embraced the therapeutic process and trusted me to encourage and challenge you to feel and explore your emotions. You demonstrated great courage and resilience by allowing yourselves to deal with your experiences rather than simply getting over them or ignoring them. Thank you for entrusting me with your healing and growth.

As I actively participated in my clients' journey toward healing, I witnessed the transformative power of allowing oneself to face and overcome discomfort. This propelled me to delve deeper into the idea of "feeling and dealing" as a path to true healing. For that, I feel immensely grateful and appreciative for this recognition. I want to express my heartfelt thanks from the depths of my heart. It is a tremendous honor to be regarded as my clients' "THERAPIST" and to play a role in their lives. As I continue on my life journey, I have come to understand, value, and appreciate the profound significance of this path. To each of you, I offer my sincere thanks. It is because of your inspiration that I've written and completed this book.

References

Ameli, Rezvan, Ninet Sinaii, María José Luna, Julia Cheringal, Brunilde Gril, and Ann Berger. "The National Institutes of Health Measure of Healing Experience of All Life Stressors (NIH-HEALS): Factor Analysis and Validation." *Plos One* 13, no. 12, (December 2018). https://doi.org/10.1371/journal.pone.0207820.

American Psychological Association Dictionary of Psychology. Accessed January 2020. http://dictionary.apa.org.

Andrade, Chittaranjan, and Rajiv Radhakrishnan. "Prayer and Healing: A Medical and Scientific Perspective on Randomized Controlled Trials." *Indian Journal of Psychiatry* 51, no. 4 (October–December 2009): 247–253. doi: 10.4103/0019-5545.58288.

Asarian, L., Gloy, V., & Geary, N. (2012). "Homeostasis." In Encyclopedia of Human Behavior (pp. 324-333). This entry provides an overview of the homeostatic mechanisms across different systems, emphasizing their role in bodily regulation.

Beck, A. T. (1976). Cognitive Therapy and the Emotional Disorder's. New York: International Universities Press.

Crawford, Cindy C., Andrew G. Sparber, and Wayne B. Jonas. "A Systematic Review of the Quality of Research on Hands-On and Distance Healing: Clinical and Laboratory Studies." *Alternative Therapies In Health And Medicine* 9 (2003): A96–104. https://pubmed.ncbi.nlm.nih.gov/12776468/.

Dersch Family Law. "Five Stages of Healing." Accessed January 2020. https://www. derschfamilylaw.com/family-law/.

Dictionary.com, accessed January 2020, Dictionary.com | Meanings & Definitions of English Words.

Glasser, William. *Counseling with Choice Theory: The New Reality Therapy*. New York: Harper Perennial, 2000.

Goleman, Daniel J. Emotional Intelligence, 10th Anniversary Edition. New York: Bantam Books, 1994.

Jung, C. G. (1959). The Archetypes and the Collective Unconscious (2nd ed., R.F.C. Hull, Trans.). Princeton, NJ: Princeton University Press.

Khan Academy, accessed January 2020, https://www.khanac-ademy.org/science/.

Kring, Ann M. & Gordon, Albert H., "Sex Differences in Emotion: Expression, Experience, and Physiology," Journal of Personality and Social Psychology 74, no. 3 (1998): 668-703.

Kübler-Ross, E. (1969). On Death and Dying. New York: Macmillan

Mayer, J. D., & Salovey, P. (1997). What is emotional intelligence? In P. Salovey & D. J. Sluyter (Eds.), Emotional development and emotional intelligence: Educational implications (pp. 3-31). New York: Basic Books.

Merriam-Webster.com, accessed January 2020, https://www.merri-am-webster.com/dictionary/validation.

New Oxford American Dictionary, Oxford University Press, 2023.

Psychology Notes HQ. (2018, May 25). The Jean Piaget Stages of Cognitive Development. Retrieved from The Psychology Notes Headquarters.

Raypole, Crystal. "Finding and Getting to Know Your Inner Child." Healthline.com. Accessed February 12, 2020. https://www.healthline.com/health/inner-child.

Salkind, Neil J., ed. *Encyclopedia of Human Development*, 3 vols. Los Angeles: Sage Publications, 2005.

Ventres, William B. "Healing." *The Annals of Family Medicine* 14, no. 1 (January 2016): 76–78. doi: 10.1370/afm.1889.

World Health Organization. *Traditional Medicine Strategy 2002-2005.* Geneva, Switzerland: World Health Organization, 2002. https://www.who.int/publications/i/item/WHO-EDM-TRM-2002.1.

About the Author

Marcella Rogers, MA, LCPC, is a seasoned professional with a wealth of experience in the field of mental and behavioral health. She earned a Master of Arts in Clinical Psychology from the Illinois School of Professional Psychology in 2001 and is a Licensed Clinical Professional Counselor (LCPC) since 2004. Marcella has dedicated her career to helping individuals discover that the answers lie within themselves.

Marcella's core belief centers around empowering her clients to tap into their innate abilities and explore the depths of their inner selves. She wants to help them process how to find, know, and search for the inner key to unlock the answers that lie within. She guides them in uncovering the underlying issues that may hinder their growth and prevent them from realizing their full potential as well as living in their truth.

With over 26 years of experience in the mental and behavioral health field, Marcella has held roles in social services agencies, psychiatric hospitals, and psychiatric rehabilitation outpatient programs. She has served thousands of individuals and families.

Her extensive background in metropolitan communities has equipped her to excel in various capacities, from working with children, teenagers, and their families to assisting adults, couples, and their broader support systems. Marcella's expertise extends to a wide range of mental health issues, including mood disorders, behavioral problems, marital challenges, life stressors, and grief and loss. Marcella's areas of specialization encompass Cognitive Behavioral Therapy (CBT), anxiety, depression, and stress and anger management.

Throughout her career, Marcella has also contributed to the field through teaching as an adjunct professor and providing supervision and training to numerous social workers and therapists. She conducts workshops, conferences, and retreats aimed at informing, educating, and assisting larger audiences.

For the past 17 years, Marcella has operated a successful private practice, Answers Lie Within, serving Chicago and surrounding communities. Her services include individual, group, family, marital, and couples counseling psychotherapy.

For more information about the services Marcella and the group practice provide, please visit www.answersliewithininc.com.